Public Affairs in Practice

PR IN PRACTICE SERIES

Public Affairs in Practice

A Practical Guide to Lobbying

Stuart Thomson
and Steve John

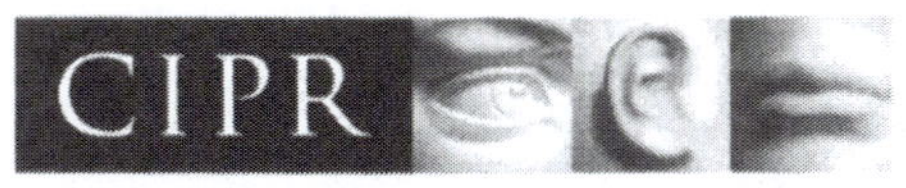

London and Philadelphia

Publisher's note

Every possible effort has been made to ensure that the information contained in this book is accurate at the time of going to press, and the publishers and authors cannot accept responsibility for any errors or omissions, however caused. No responsibility for loss or damage occasioned to any person acting, or refraining from action, as a result of the material in this publication can be accepted by the editor, the publisher or any of the authors.

First published in Great Britain and the United States in 2007 by Kogan Page Limited
Reprinted in 2007

120 Pentonville Road
London N1 9JN
United Kingdom
www.kogan-page.co.uk

525 South 4th Street, #241
Philadelphia PA 19147
USA

ISBN-10 0 7494 4472 X
ISBN-13 978 0 7494 4472 3

British Library Cataloguing-in-Publication Data

A CIP record for this book is available from the British Library.

Library of Congress Cataloging-in-Publication Data

Thomson, Stuart.
Public affairs in practice / Stuart Thomson and Steve John.
p. cm.
ISBN 0-7494-4472-X
1. Lobbying. 2. Pressure groups. I. John, Steve, 1972– II. Title.
JF1118.J64 2007
324'.4–cc22

2006016468

Typeset by JS Typesetting Ltd, Porthcawl, Mid Glamorgan
Printed and bound in Great Britain by MPG Books Ltd, Bodmin, Cornwall

Stuart would like to dedicate this book to Alex and William.
Steve would like to dedicate this book to his mother, Helen.

Contents

Foreword by Senator George Mitchell *xi*
Foreword *xiii*
Preface *xv*

1. Introduction **1**
Public affairs in practice 2
What is lobbying? 3
Lobbying or public affairs? 4
How the UK public affairs industry has changed 5
What difference does public affairs make? 7
Public affairs around the globe 8
Getting into public affairs 11
Early stages 14
Codes of conduct 15
Overall 16

2. The art of lobbying **19**
Why lobby? 20
Monitoring 21
What do you want to do? 24
How policy is made in the UK 25
Policy 33
How to lobby 39

Contact programme 40
Meetings 45
Local government 47
Scotland 48
Wales 50
Europe 51
Global institutions 55
General rules 57

3. Reputation and the media **63**
Media relations 64
Crisis management 70

4. Managing issues **83**
Get to the heart of the issue 83
Building the evidence 86
Think tanks 88
Economic consultancies 90
Business schools 91
Polling organizations 92
Building support 93
Conclusion 99

5. Stakeholder relations **105**
The value of stakeholders 106
Identify your stakeholders 107
Understanding your stakeholders 109
Engaging your stakeholders 111
Planning communications 112
Summary 114

6. Corporate social responsibility **121**
Definitions 122
Measuring CSR 123
The growth of CSR 124
Why CSR? 125
The role of government 128
Impact of CSR on public affairs 130
Conclusion 134

7. Conclusion **141**
On a personal level 142
Future trends and developments 143

Overall 146
Public affairs – a checklist 147

Appendix – codes of conduct *149*
CIPR *149*
APPC *150*
PRCA *152*
EPACA *154*
EULobby.net *155*
SEAP *158*

Index *161*

Foreword

Public affairs is about more than just lobbying politicians. At its heart is the ability to understand politics, decision-making, government infrastructures and policymaking. You need to know what makes the media tick and how it impacts on politicians. To do all this you need to understand the society in which you operate.

Those involved in public affairs have to be able to communicate with a wide variety of audiences, and know what those audiences need and expect. It is no good going to, for instance, politicians, and being unable to answer their questions simply because you had not anticipated them. A failure to understand will simply lead to failure - guaranteed. As a politician, I have been on the receiving end of lobbying and the quality varies widely.

This book fills a gap by offering practical help to those coming into the industry, and perhaps even for a few seasoned professionals as well. It explains what those in public affairs should look out for in a very practical and real way, from understanding the policymaking structures to the tools at their disposal.

This book will enhance the continuing development of a professional industry that can bring very real and valuable benefits to those who want their voices to be heard.

Senator George Mitchell

Foreword

To many public relations practitioners the world of public affairs is an unknown and murky one. In this book Stuart Thomson and Steve John have done and excellent job in demystifying both the role and practice of public affairs.

It is important that such a book is in the series. If democracy is to flourish and if we are to live in a society where our legislators are informed, it is vital that they a provided with accurate, timely and comprehensive information from a variety of sources, only then they make informed decisions. The same, of course, applies to all of us, but it is especially important for those who frame the society in which we all live. There are dangers here in that those organizations with power, influence and resources and who, therefore, have a 'big voice', may drown out the small, but legitimate voices. One of the principal benefits of a vibrant public relations industry is that it can help ensure that a voice is given to those unable to speak for themselves: witness to this claim are the innumerable pressure groups for animal rights, indigenous peoples, those with disabilities and a myriad of other 'minority interests'. However, it would be naïve to claim that all groups have equal access to a 'share of the voice', they clearly do not.

This is one of the main reasons why this book exists. It provides an excellent introduction to what lobbying is and the various processes it entails. It gives detailed information on the various legislative bodies in the UK and overseas and a clear route map for how to engage with them. Importantly, it doesn't stop there. It points out the importance of involving other stakeholders as advocates and introduces a vital ethical dimension by covering the duty of organizations to be good corporate citizens.

Thomson and John have peppered the big picture with practical 'how to' advice. Helpfully, they have also indicated how, if the lobbying career tempts you, you might break into an area of public relations that is challenging, rewarding and intrinsically worthwhile if done ethically and with public interest in mind. This book should be on every inspiring lobbyist's shelf.

Anne Gregory
Series Editor

Preface

Public affairs is still a relatively young profession in the United Kingdom but is increasing in importance as the value and worth of reputations are recognized in business and among NGOs and charities. The profession is constantly changing and evolving as are the skills needed to deliver an effective and comprehensive public affairs strategy.

We believe that public affairs is an important part of the political lexicon and can deliver benefits to all those involved. If conducted properly it can deliver better policies that can benefit all parts of society – individual citizens, their representative bodies and organizations, as well as business.

For those entering the industry there is not currently a book available that helps them to learn about the 'dos and don'ts' or what is expected of them. We have brought our experience, and that of others, to write *Public Affairs in Practice*, which endeavours to be that book.

There are many people we would like to thank for helping us to deliver this book but chief amongst these is Matthew Davies who has played a fundamental part in the delivery of our work. His input has been invaluable and his helpful questioning has meant that we have had to think through our arguments and write them in a way that those new to the industry will be able to understand.

Matthew works for Upstream, the government affairs and media relations practice of DLA Piper. We too both worked for Upstream before we moved to pastures new. Whilst there, Lord Tim Clement-Jones, chairman of the practice, was supportive of our ambition to write this book. Other colleagues, Suzy Awford, Kajsa Stenström and Patrik Karlsson, all played a role and helped improve the book. The new pastures for Stuart is as a Senior Public Affairs Adviser at Bircham Dyson Bell, the London law firm and parliamentary agents. Steve is now Director of Government Relations at PepsiCo.

We also want to say a very big 'thank you' to Jonathan Bracken who took the time and trouble to read our manuscript from a practitioner's perspective to ensure that we make some sense throughout. Jonathan is a partner and Head of Public Policy at Bircham Dyson Bell, the law firm and parliamentary agents, and is an expert in the fields of public affairs, legislative drafting and regulatory policy. Jonathan is also Chair of the CIPR Government Affairs Group and has over 20 years' experience of working on high-profile lobbying campaigns and public affairs projects in the United Kingdom, Europe and the United States. We are grateful for his valuable input.

To have someone as esteemed as Senator George Mitchell write the foreword for this book is a real honour. Senator Mitchell is best-known in the United Kingdom for chairing the Northern Ireland peace talks that led to the accord ending decades of violence. He spent 14 years in the Senate and is widely admired across the political spectrum. He is also the Chairman of the Walt Disney Company and the author of several books.

To all those who have contributed tips and those who allowed us to use their work as case studies, we say thank you. By sharing best practice we hope the profession will continue to develop.

For the supportive comments on the book cover we would like to thank Alastair Stewart, a wonderfully experienced and respected journalist; Stephen Twigg, Director of the Foreign Policy Centre, a former government minister and former Labour MP for Enfield Southgate; Ed Vaizey MP, the Conservative Member for Wantage and a former lobbyist; and, once again, Jonathan Bracken.

Gro Elin Hansen, at the CIPR, agreed that we could write this book as part of their *In Practice* series and we hope that our work complements the work of its other authors. Pauline Goodwin, Publishing Director at Kogan Page, deserves a special mention for giving us the go-ahead with the book and for agreeing that one of Britain's foremost publishers would put our work into print. Annie Knight, Development Editor at Kogan Page, made sure that we made any changes needed, and Helen Savill, Project Editor, kept us to deadline! Anne Gregory, Series Editor also provided some useful comments on our work.

On a personal level, Stuart would like to thank his wife, Alex, and son, William – a wonderful and supportive family who do not mind me slaving over a computer for hours on end. My mother (Maureen), father (Bill) and brother (Iain) also encourage me and have done so for countless years – this is your fault!

Steve would like to thank his family for their long-standing and continuing support, patience and encouragement.

We hope that you find the book to be an enjoyable and useful read.

1

Introduction

The lobbying industry is, to put it mildly, not viewed favourably and does not enjoy a favourable press. Partly through its own actions and partly as a result of spin levelled against it, lobbying is not an industry about which many have a good understanding. Few have any real idea about what lobbyists do and why they do it. Knowledge of public affairs is even more limited.

So what do lobbyists do and what is public affairs? Why should anyone need to know what the industry does? Most importantly, what impact does the industry have and should it be welcomed, by governments, businesses and citizens?

This book aims to shed light on the public affairs industry by explaining what it does and why, what its impact is and why people make use of it. This is the first book that explores the methods used by the industry to make an impact and in so doing it will explode some of the myths.

By untangling the web that is public affairs, each chapter will provide practical advice and examples alongside an explanation of the tactics. We hope that this will be of use to students eager to know more, existing practitioners looking to keep up to date, as well as those new to the industry just eager to learn.

PUBLIC AFFAIRS IN PRACTICE

This book will provide a clear and accessible explanation of public affairs, looking at the tools involved in delivering a public affairs programme and examining each area of public affairs in turn. It must, however, be stressed that public affairs is constantly evolving. Public affairs grows with business and political behaviour. It now includes corporate social responsibility (CSR) and elements of corporate governance only recently taken on by the business community because of the impact they have on reputation with political and media audiences. No doubt in years to come there will be new skills required in delivering public affairs and anyone involved, including students of the industry, should be ready to recognize these and adapt to them.

Each chapter deals with a component part of public affairs and explores it in detail. As with other books in the CIPR's *PR in Practice* series, the book has been made as practical as possible and includes a number of case studies to ensure that readers, whatever their perspective or experience, can treat this as a 'how to' guide.

In the rest of the Introduction to this book we provide a brief overview of lobbying and public affairs in the United Kingdom. We go on to examine how the public affairs industry in the UK has grown and, importantly, what the benefits of a public affairs programme are. There is a description of public affairs in other countries, particularly the United States. We then try to describe ways of getting into the industry, the skills you need to be successful, how to secure a job and, once there, what you can expect from your early years in public affairs. The introduction ends with a discussion about the importance of codes of conduct in the industry.

Chapter 2 deals with lobbying and is the longest chapter in the book. Despite the changes in the job specification for those involved in public affairs, lobbying remains at its heart. For this reason we look at it in some detail, from what benefits lobbying can bring and how to maintain a watch on parliament and other relevant parts of the political process, through to how to lobby. This is, as you can imagine, far from straightforward and there is a necessary examination of the policymaking process in Westminster to help better understand where the pressure points are in the system. The chapter looks at lobbying local government, Scotland, Wales, Europe and global institutions as all these require their own forms of lobbying.

Chapter 3 moves on to the role of the media in public affairs and deals with it in two parts. The first suggests ways in which a positive relationship can be developed with the media, in all its forms, and how to engage with journalists. The second part of the chapter is concerned with crisis management and how your organization should deal with problems when they arise. The maintenance of a positive reputation, as mentioned above, is crucial when dealing with political audiences.

Chapter 4 broadens into a discussion about the management of issues and how to understand, build, develop and present them in a way that will secure support for your cause or campaign. This includes building evidence for your issue and support that can help secure policy change.

Chapter 5 examines stakeholder relations and the role that an organization's stakeholders play in public affairs campaigns. From identifying your stakeholders through to understanding their motivations and how to engage with them, the chapter aims to show how valuable your stakeholders are. The chapter ends with a short discussion of planning communications, which is an area of public affairs that calls for the use of stakeholder relations.

Chapter 6 looks at the growing issue of corporate social responsibility (CSR) and its increasing importance in public affairs. Starting with definitions of CSR along with its measurement and growth, the chapter goes on to discuss how government is dealing with CSR and how this has impacted on public affairs campaigns.

In the Conclusion to the book, we look at how you can develop your career in public affairs and then suggest some future trends and developments.

WHAT IS LOBBYING?

Lobbying has grown in importance. In the United Kingdom, the industry continues to grow with new entrants all the time. Companies have their own 'in-house' teams and use a plethora of consultants to add value and skills to augment their existing teams. Academic institutions are now running courses in lobbying and it is beginning to be recognized in courses that teach undergraduates about the political system. Lobbying is now a profession, albeit formally unrecognized, that businesses use and value and one that people want to enter but without always knowing what to expect and what it really is.

Lobbying can be seen as:

> any action designed to influence the actions of the institutions of government. That means it covers all parts of central and local government and other public bodies, both in the UK and internationally. Its scope includes legislation, regulatory and policy decisions, and negotiations on public sector contacts or grants.[1]

Commercial lobbyists will seek to influence political and policy decisions on behalf of their clients; an 'in-house' lobbyist will do the same but only for the organization for which they work. Lobbying on UK national policy decisions will focus quite narrowly on the political institutions and actors in Westminster and Whitehall.

> Lobbying is an important part of the democratic process. Always has been. Always will be. There is nothing wrong with paying consultants for political advice. Businessmen, charities and trade associations are not experts on the political system so they pay people who are.[2]

There remains a general mistrust of lobbyists and it is believed by many that they in some way distort the political process. Politicians and civil servants alike are not keen to admit that they meet with lobbyists or that they welcome the knowledge that a well-briefed lobbyist can bring. The public affairs industry has though, on several and high-profile occasions, been led astray by its 'members' who have tried to oversell themselves and their contacts in order to maximize their revenue. As a consequence, there are now a number of codes of conduct championed by professional bodies such as the CIPR and the PRCA in the United Kingdom and a European code; alongside these stand codes of conduct for politicians at national and local levels. These are all designed to ensure that lobbyists and politicians behave in a manner consistent with public expectations of probity. It was only as recently as the end of the 1990s that Corinne Souza was able to write 'commercial lobbying, at the moment at least, is for the most part home to those with little initiative and not enough scruples.'[3]

LOBBYING OR PUBLIC AFFAIRS?

The name of this book is *Public Affairs in Practice* and yet so far we have not made clear why instead the book is not called 'Lobbying in Practice'.

Public affairs goes further than lobbying. Public affairs is not just about what goes on in Westminster and Whitehall but also about working with other policymaking or influencing bodies such as regulators, commercial bodies and an organization's stakeholders. All of these are important in helping to achieve a desired policy outcome. Most importantly, a public affairs consultant recognizes the importance of the media – broadcast and print. The media can reflect or shape public opinion and politicians take notice of what it says; it applies pressure on them. The media can, therefore, be a valuable advocate for a policy so a public affairs professional needs to be able to work with the media.

In what is probably the authoritative study of the numbers involved in public affairs in the United Kingdom, Milner estimates that there are somewhere between 600 and 800 public affairs consultancy practitioners in the UK. By looking at earlier figures he also suggests that the industry has doubled in size since 1991 with consultancy fee income estimated with 'extreme caution' at over £60.5m.[4] Overall, if one accepts Heinz *et al*'s contention that for every consultant there are four 'in-house' counterparts, that means that there are around 3,000 public affairs practioners in the UK states Milner.[5]

There has been a growing recognition of the role that an organization's reputation can play. A good reputation in the media and amongst politicians can help your argument; likewise a poor reputation can hinder your case. Public affairs has entered the realm of reputation management (maintaining a good image) and all that that entails – from an organization's corporate social responsibility policies through to the way in which it deals with difficult business decisions such as job losses.

Most straightforwardly, lobbying is about Westminster and Whitehall but public affairs is about politics as a whole. Very few issues or problems will ever be solved simply by employing lobbyists, ie simply by concentrating on Westminster and Whitehall to achieve an outcome. Instead, a successful campaign needs to address many different audiences. Only in these circumstances can success be achieved. Public affairs is taking over from lobbying and there are many different parts to public affairs, each of which needs to be explored, as this book does.

Public affairs has increasingly been used in an era where companies have become more professional and less reliant on old networks of contacts. Organizations can no longer simply rely on 'who they know'; the quality of their argument is fundamental.

HOW THE UK PUBLIC AFFAIRS INDUSTRY HAS CHANGED

The history of lobbying can be traced back for many hundreds of years but in modern times it has particularly evolved over the past 20. In this time, public affairs has become less about trading upon contacts and links into a government and has made significant strides to become increasingly professionalized. Initially dominated in the modern period by several large personalities such as Ian Greer, a well-connected Conservative who spoke openly about his level of contacts in the government, the main companies in lobbying were led from the front by their charismatic leaders. These companies were close to the then Conservative Government, which had been in power for a number of years. These very close links became a liability.

Ian Greer Associates became embroiled in the 'cash for questions' scandal in 1994 that rocked the Conservative Government. Money changed hands for MPs asking questions in parliament as part of lobbying campaigns. Graham Riddick MP and David Treddinnick MP, both Conservative, were found to have accepted money for such purposes. However, even more high-profile was the case of the Conservative MP for Tatton, Neil Hamilton. Hamilton accepted gifts from the boss of Harrods, Mohammed Al Fayed. Al Fayed believed that the acceptance of gifts was in exchange for political and parliamentary activity on his behalf. This and other allegations of sleaze eventually, in part, contributed to the downfall of the Conservative Government and the historic scale of its defeat in the 1997 general election. However, it also showed, to many, that the lobbying industry did not behave in an ethical manner and the whole of the industry was tarred with the same brush.

Great strides have been made to try to improve the image of public affairs, for instance through the introduction of codes of conduct, but in many ways the whole industry is still forced to act in a rather defensive manner and remains on the back foot. This is a major challenge in an era where reputation is increasingly important. If the activity of a company's lobbyists is likely to cause damage to its reputation then why would it employ them?

The economic downturn around 2000 caused a shift in the structure of the industry. Until that point, whilst several of the 'large personalities' had gone from the scene, it remained dominated by several large firms such as GJW, GPC, Citigate and Shandwick. Each of these firms had around 40–50 consultants with teams specializing in areas such as local government and planning, mergers and acquisitions etc. The economic downturn meant that there was less work available for these firms and many were forced to reduce staff numbers. Rather than leave the industry, many of these consultants started their own firms often specializing in particular business sectors. Reduced fee income also left many independent companies and sole traders open to takeover. A period of consolidation took place with many firms being swallowed up by big public relations companies. Overall there is now a greater level of competition in the industry than there was 10 years ago.

Lobbying has also been one of the services offered by public relations firms. Many of these firms claim to offer full communications service capabilities and, therefore, include communicating with political audiences, ie lobbying, as part of that service. In this sense, lobbying is part of the wider communications service offering. There are now really no firms that just lobby.

Following its election in 1997, the Labour Government introduced devolution for Scotland and Wales and this brought with it a further change in the, now, public affairs industry. Several operations sprung up in Edinburgh and Cardiff, some of them run by former Westminster lobbyists returning home to start their own operations, whilst other operations were the offices of larger firms that wanted to offer a service across all parliaments/assemblies in the United Kingdom. The public affairs markets in both Scotland and Wales remain small. The Labour Government is also committed to holding referendums in the regions of England that would offer them their own assemblies. If these were to be passed then there would be a further devolution of power and again the public affairs industry would have to adapt to the decision-making structure.

As the importance of the European Union, its legislation and regulation, has increased for member states, public affairs firms have had to demonstrate a capability in Brussels so that they can influence policy.

WHAT DIFFERENCE DOES PUBLIC AFFAIRS MAKE?

This is a question that needs to be posed as many companies do not see the benefit of engaging in public affairs activity and, aside from any other benefits, believe that it does not add to their 'bottom line'. This is understandable. Many in the industry have struggled to communicate what the benefits are and how they can be measured. Being introduced to policy advisers may be useful to a company but what difference does it make?

Public affairs can:

- protect an organization from the perceived threat of a new policy initiative or regulation, such as the impact that a new regulatory body may have;
- offer protection against adverse comment being made about the company by government, politicians or others in the industry by being in a position to keep them informed;
- offer assistance in spotting new market opportunities as government policy changes, for instance on the use of information technology;
- protect and enhance the reputation of the organization, as a good name will stand you in better stead if you need to campaign against a measure;
- assist in the building of support through a greater network of contacts;
- raise the profile of the organization;
- protect the organization against the public affairs activity of a competitor;
- lessen the possibility of adverse action being taken by government or a regulator as they are better informed about your activity;
- ensure that personal reputations are enhanced.

Far from being a distortion of the political process, a criticism made by some, many politicians and civil servants require assistance in formulating policy. Time and resources are always limited and many policymakers welcome the opinions and direction of outside bodies, often before a formal consultation stage is reached. For a politician, such outside assistance may help to avoid a damaging incident or fallout if they understand the full consequences of the proposed action; for a civil servant the assistance may mean the difference between well-framed and comprehensive legislation or a bill that is full of holes and could reflect badly on them and their department, with the associated possibility of a fall in funding as the department is 'punished' for its failures.

It is also important to remember that public affairs activity is not just undertaken by private sector companies but also charities, non-governmental organizations (NGOs), trade unions, local authorities, public sector bodies, such as the police, education establishments and health authorities, and individuals. The corporate sector is often criticized for lobbying government whilst these others remain free from such criticism. Also NGOs are able to lobby for what they perceive to be the 'public interest' whilst companies are accused of lobbying for their own sectional and commercial interests that may actually be in the public interest. This provides NGOs with a built-in advantage, namely public support (real or imagined) that can be called upon, whereas companies are always in the position of having to prove to political audiences that they have public support.

It is true that often the corporate sector may devote more resources to a public affairs campaign but, as we will show in this book, money does not guarantee success. A successful public affairs campaign is all about how well you explain your problem, the quality of the argument – how it is set out, explained, justified, supported – and, importantly, how the problem can be solved.

PUBLIC AFFAIRS AROUND THE GLOBE

Public affairs exists to various degrees across the world. In the United States, lobbying is a much more widely accepted business practice than it is elsewhere and its benefits are better understood. Yet the power of companies is coming in for increased criticism especially under President Bush, and scandals such as the one involving Jack Abramoff, who received a six-year jail term for fraud, have tarnished the lobbying industry.[6] The links between the political élite and business in the United States is much closer than it has traditionally been in the United Kingdom, with one simple example being the number of business people who go on to hold senior governmental positions in the US. The major factor in the link between business and politicians in the US has to do with the funding of political campaigns. Through Political Action Committees (PACs), individual donations and corporate donations, companies provide candidates with very large sums of money and continue to exert an influence on the elected representative once in office through the threat of the withdrawal of funding.

The nature of the public affairs industry varies largely between countries. In the United States, lobbyists were traditionally part of law firms, but now this too has begun to change as politics has become a profession and not just a vocation, alongside a move towards grass roots public affairs carried out by not-for-profit bodies and utilizing individual citizens. Public policy lawyers used to engage with politicians on a day to day basis and this was, to a large extent, why they undertook lobbying on behalf of their clients. They also built up an enviable amount of specialist knowledge that policymakers were interested in utilizing. The lobbying firms themselves tend to be very large in terms of turnover and numbers of employees, and based in Washington. Quinn Gillespie and Barbour Griffith & Rogers are just two of the firms that are part of the boom in lobbying that has seen the number of registered lobbyists in Washington more than double since 2000 to over 34,750. Some have even suggested that the number of industry participants in Washington, DC has reached 100,000.[7] Lobbyists in the US make much of their connections with politicians and many are former elected representatives. The large part of an American lobbyist's sales pitch to a potential client is on the basis of his or her connections with the president and Congress.[8]

Doug Pinkham, President, Public Affairs Council

Many people think all you need is a high-powered lobbyist to get things done in Washington, DC. But members of Congress are much more responsive to constituents than they are to lobbyists. Because House members are running for re-election every two years, they are always taking the pulse of voters. That's why 'grass roots' communication has grown so dramatically. One of the most effective – and underutilized – ways to build grass roots support is local media outreach. Visits to local newspapers and doing radio talk show interviews can give momentum to an issue. A congressman pays more attention to those media outlets than to the *Washington Post* or the *New York Times*.

Toby Moffett, Senior Counselor, The Livingston Group

At the end of the day facts and reputation still matter more than anything else. As most people who observe the US political system or practice within it know, the system has been corrupted, at least in spirit, by the almost fanatical focus on campaign contributions, on political survival, on keeping incumbents in office by continuing a system of drawing district representation lines so as to prevent challengers from having much of a chance.

But I find that most representatives, regardless of party affiliation or ideology, try to do the right thing, try very hard to gather facts, make sober judgments as to what positions to take.

So having your facts in order in crucial. And believing in whatever you are representing or advocating is too.

That's where reputation comes in. If you present bad facts or if it's apparent you are merely going through the motions in your 'advocacy', your reputation suffers. And with it your business.

Brussels, as everyone recognizes, is an increasingly important source of legislation and regulation for member states of the European Union. As will be described later in this book, the EU's legislative process is very different from that of the United Kingdom and takes place over a considerably longer period. UK public affairs firms increasingly have to demonstrate a capability in Brussels. Firms need to be able to show that they can lobby on EU legislation before it comes anywhere near the United Kingdom. Public affairs firms in Brussels tend to be part of much larger organizations, ie the Brussels office of such an outfit. Otherwise they are smaller, independent companies who often have partnership arrangements with firms in member states, such as the UK, to allow the referral of work.

The lobbying industry in other European member states varies quite considerably. The new accession members have no real industry, whereas the formerly small German public affairs market is now making greater use of its historical role and taking advantage of the 'incorporation of innovative media and PR strategies into more traditional lobbying strategies *inside* the political system'[9] (our italics). In France, it is claimed that there is no real lobbying industry. Whilst this is, in essence, correct it is the case that lobbying tends to be undertaken through informal networks and contacts rather than professional firms. This is assisted by the education system in France whereby the vast majority of top business people and those involved in politics, either in elected position or in the civil service, went to one of several top universities, certain members of the *grand écoles* – such as the Ecole Polytechnique, Ecole Nationale Supérieure and the Ecole Nationale d'Administration (ENA). In the Scandinavian countries public affairs is beginning to grow and develop in an embryonic form.

Several firms in the UK, and global firms, are now looking to fill in the blanks in this somewhat patchy picture by aiming to deliver public affairs services not only in the UK and Brussels but across all EU member states. In a sense as business becomes more international then so too does public affairs and this is currently best seen in the growth and development of China as a market for public affairs activity.

GETTING INTO PUBLIC AFFAIRS

As can be seen above, the public affairs industry is growing and so people have made the decision that public affairs is the career that they want to pursue then they must take steps to get involved in the industry. There are several traditional routes into public affairs but it is essential that candidates are able to show a clear commitment to politics, communications and the media on their CVs.

This means that during your time in education, especially further and higher education, they should build skills and experience that will be useful in public affairs. If you want to get into the industry you could consider:

- Working in the office of an MP – this will provide a very solid grounding in politics, the demands of politicians and how politics really works. In addition, working for an MP can also be a high-pressure environment and there are many similarities with public affairs!
- Assisting a local councillor – again good for building a knowledge of working politics.
- Securing a secondment in Westminster or Whitehall – these can sometimes be organized by your academic institution.
- Working for a public affairs company – many take on students over the holidays, usually post-18 only, and some may pay you or give you an allowance for the time spent with them.
- Finding work in the media – many media outlets, especially at local level, will let you spend time with them.
- Working for the political parties – the political parties often take students on work placement schemes.
- Getting involved in student politics – student politics can provide an understanding and network that is unavailable to others.
- Approaching think tanks – many have specialist intern positions and would happy to receive CVs from potential interns.
- Trying third party organizations – look at opportunities with pressure groups, NGOs or business groups. Experience can come from a number of sources, not just the political parties.

As well as this 'on the job' experience there are also an increasing number of courses or parts of courses that teach public affairs. One of the best known of these courses in the UK is offered by Brunel University, which offers an internship as part of the course.

Your aim is to spend time in an environment where you will learn and develop skills that will prove useful in your chosen career. Consider also other skills that could prove useful:

- languages – especially if you want to work in Brussels;
- technology – a good working knowledge of information technology is essential;
- communications – personal and interpersonal;
- writing – you must be able to write well, assimilate details, summarize them and deliver to deadlines;
- oral – listen and interact with others;
- presentation – stand up in front of a group of people and deliver a presentation;
- initiative – be a self-motivator;
- team – work well with others.

When you have developed these skills and built a quality CV, you must then ensure that your CV and covering letter are appropriately tailored to the opportunity to which you are applying. There are many styles and format of CV but it should be no longer than two sides of A4 and must include two quality referees. Remember that your CV may be kept by those you send it to for a period of time and it is worth sending speculative letters and CVs. Details of public affairs firms can be found in:

- *Directory of Political Lobbying*;
- *Dod's Parliamentary Companion*;
- Association of Professional Political Consultants website (www.appc.org.uk);
- *PR Week* 'Black Book';
- *PRCA Yearbook*;
- *Government Affairs Group (GAG) Handbook*;
- *Who's Who In Public Affairs*;
- CIPR website (www.cipr.co.uk).

Consult the careers service at your school, college, or higher education institution. Some public affairs companies advertise positions through these offices and some actively ask for public affairs firms to send details of opportunities to them.

Once your education is complete, whether you have gained experience or not, some of the above opportunities will remain open to you. Yet other opportunities may arise, for instance a *stage* in Brussels (time spent with the Commission or a directorate) is a favoured way of gaining experience. Another idea would be to apply for a graduate traineeship with a public affairs firm. The chances of getting a permanent job after completing such a traineeship are high and it gives you a chance to prove yourself. These placements can last from three months to a year and can pay well or hardly anything. Some also include time spent with other organizations to help you build your range of skills.

Make friends in the industry and speak to them about entry; they may know of opportunities or will let you know if there are certain areas where your CV is deficient. Not all opportunities are advertised and some come about simply because of persistence.

There are, however, a number of places that you can look for a job, placement or traineeship:

- Work 4 an MP – a website dedicated to opportunities with MPs and the industry in general (www.w4mp.org);
- PubAffairs – a network of young public affairs practitioners that circulates details of opportunities by e-mail (www.pubaffairs.org);
- *PR Week* – the weekly trade publication for the PR industry including public affairs (www.prweek.com);
- *Public Affairs News* – the main trade magazine for the industry and a very good way to get to know your way around the main companies, individuals and work (www.publicaffairsnews.com);
- Electus Start – a site that offers details of opportunities available and sources of advice (www.electus-start.com);
- the *Guardian* – media section (Monday) and Jobs & Money (Saturday) (www.guardian.co.uk);
- *The House Magazine* – situations vacant at the end of magazine (www.housemag.co.uk);
- Interns Network – aimed more towards those who are already interns and are looking at stepping into a public affairs role (www.internsnetwork.org.uk);
- CIPR website – the website of the CIPR carries job adverts (www.cipr.co.uk/jobs).

Some recruitment consultants also hear about first-time jobs and it is worth speaking to them. Again they may also give you advice on entry into the industry and companies that you could approach. They have their ears to the ground.

Gavin Ellwood, Director, Ellwood and Atfield

Planning a career in public affairs means thinking strategically, that is thinking three to seven years ahead. This industry continues to undergo rapid change, and predicting what it will look like in the future is difficult. However, your career won't go far wrong if you follow three rules:

Rule 1. Don't be siloed. Keep abreast of developments in your sister disciplines especially media relations, social responsibility and policy development.

Rule 2. Measure your success. Public affairs can measurably influence the success of an organization; make sure your work does just that.

Rule 3. Manage your reputation. Understand the importance of your reputation as well as that of the organization or individual you represent.

EARLY STAGES

As in the early part of any career, once you enter the industry, you will be expected to do a lot of the groundwork upon which all public affairs rely. You must be prepared to learn the basics of public affairs long before you have direct exposure to clients (if you work for a consultancy). Your typical working day will include:

- monitoring parliamentary activity through *Hansard*;
- monitoring the activity of government departments and other organizations, for instance by regular checks on websites;
- monitoring e-mails and press releases;
- writing e-mails to clients detailing the monitoring;
- preparing background research papers on issues, companies or sectors;
- preparing lists of opinion formers (politicians etc);
- attending parliamentary committees and writing reports on the proceedings;
- answering questions from clients about parliamentary activity or researching queries that they may have.

You will be faced with a steep learning curve and many words and phrases will be new to you, for instance:

- 'creds' – short for credentials, a prospective client may ask you for these to detail your experience and services;

- 'proposal' – you will deliver a full proposal to a prospective client with ideas about how you can help them;
- 'pitch' – similar to a proposal in that it can contain ideas for a client but is normally in presentation form, principally PowerPoint.

Other phrases such as 'briefing paper', more specific to public affairs, will be explained throughout this book.

Also on entering the industry, be familiar with the career path. Typically this is: account executive, account manager, account director, director. Sometimes there will be 'in-between' stages with the words 'junior' or 'senior' before each title. The further you progress the more the emphasis will be placed on contact with clients, strategic advice and also new business and service development.

Aside from experience, you can also build your career through training. A number of courses are offered, particularly by the CIPR. These courses cover a range of relevant skills sets from writing pitches through to networking or media relations. The CIPR also runs a diploma for those interested in gaining a formal qualification. In particular, the CIPR runs two courses aimed at public affairs, an 'Introduction to Public Affairs' and 'Influencing Public Policy'.

Be sure to get to know the industry more intimately when you secure your first job. A good starting point is continuing to read *Public Affairs News*, *PR Week* and *Profile* (the CIPR magazine). They will help you to familiarize yourself with the main players in the industry and the types of places where consultancies secure work. Both *PR Week* and *Profile* also carry case studies that will show you best practice in the industry from the outset.

CODES OF CONDUCT

Following the Ian Greer scandal (see page 5) and other revelations such as claims by lobbyists of 'insider' status and an ability to know the key decision-makers and politicians 'intimately', the public affairs industry was not seen to be behaving in an ethical manner.

As a result of this, a greater emphasis was placed on ethical behaviour and a number of codes of conduct have been written and updated since this time. These codes set out clearly the rules to which those that sign up to them must adhere. Chief amongst these are the APPC, PRCA and, in a more general PR context, the CIPR. Enhanced codes of conduct are also being considered in Europe to strengthen the existing codes. Not only has the European lobbyists' professional organization, the Society of European Affairs Professionals, recently strengthened its codes (see www.seap.

eu.org/code.php) but also current anti-fraud commissioner, Siim Kallas, has announced sweeping plans to address the lack of binding transparency rules for lobbyists operating in Brussels.[10] A selection of the existing codes in the UK and EU, is provided in the Appendix to this book.

The UK government has made a series of attempts to clarify its relationships with interested bodies. The Committee on Standards in Public Life was established in 1994 to be an 'ethical workshop'. Through inquiries, reports and research into public attitudes, the committee fulfils this role. Its first chair, Lord Nolan, a distinguished judge, now gives his name to the rules to which elected politicians are meant to adhere, the 'Nolan rules' (see www.public-standards.gov.uk/).

As a result of the committee's recommendations, the Office of the Parliamentary Commissioner for Standards was set up to maintain a watch on the conduct of MPs (www.parliament.uk/about_commons/pcfs.cfm).

In addition, the Cabinet Office has published guidance for civil service contact with lobbyists (www.cabinetoffice.gov.uk/propriety_and_ethics/civil_service/lobbyists.asp). There is a ministerial code, a code for special advisers, a code for public appointments and clearly established codes for local government and for contact with councillors.

OVERALL

This book will help you to build the skills that you need to be successful in public affairs whether you have a role 'in-house' or in consultancy. Your actual public affairs skills will vary little between the two but if you are 'in-house' then you need to have a good understanding of working with colleagues from all parts of the business who may not understand or appreciate your role. You will need to be able to explain what you do, why you are speaking to your colleagues or asking for information and why they should assist you. There are, of course, other differences between consultancy and 'in-house' activities but the need to be able to work closely with a wider range of colleagues from across different parts of the business is a key differentiator. Working 'in-house' means that you concentrate solely on the issues relevant to your organization, not those for a range of clients, sometimes drawn from across diverse sectors, which you must do as a consultant.

Welcome to public affairs!

Endnotes

1. Miller, C (2000) *Politico's Guide to Lobbying*, Politico's Publishing, London, p 4

2. Souza, C and Dale, I (1999) *Directory of Political Lobbying 1999-2000*, Politico's Publishing, London, p 1
3. Souza, C (1998) *So You Want to be a Lobbyist?*, Politico's Publishing, 1998, p xi
4. Milner, K (2006) *The Growth of Consultancy Lobbying Firms in the UK*, Leeds Business School; and Chandiramani, R (2006) PA firms enjoy surge in public body contracts, *PR Week*, 26 January
5. Milner cites Heinz, J, Laumann, E, Nelson, R and Salisbury, R (1993) *The Hollow Core*, Harvard University Press, Cambridge, USA
6. For a highly critical view of Bush's links to private companies see Moore, M (2004) *Dude, Where's My Country?*, Penguin, London
7. Harrison, S (2000) *Public Relations – An Introduction* as cited in Milner, K (2006) *The Growth of Consultancy Lobbying Firms in the UK*, Leeds Business School
8. For a short overview of the US industry see Jeffrey H. Birnbaum (2005) The road to riches is called K Street, *Washington Post*, 22 June
9. Bastow, S (2000) Public affairs in Germany, *Public Affairs Newsletter*, August, p 7
10. http://www.euractiv.com/Article?tcmuri=tcm:29-136454-16&type=News

2

The art of lobbying

Lobbying is constantly changing. This is because lobbying is fundamentally concerned with political processes, which requires an engagement with the institutions of government as well as politicians themselves. Political agendas and requirements vary over time, so the tools of lobbying have to change as well. Echoing former Labour Prime Minister Harold Wilson's phrase 'a week is a long time in politics', one can equally say 'a week is a long time in lobbying'.

For those engaged in lobbying there is no substitute for an understanding of the workings of government, of whatever level, but this must be combined with a feel and understanding of the politics behind the decision-making process. Many of those involved in lobbying have often worked for an MP or MEP, been involved in local politics or trade unions, been active politically or employed in a body of government, eg the civil service.[1] Lobbyists come from this background not simply because of the contacts such work provides but because of the understanding they gain – an understanding of the formal decision-making processes but enhanced by an understanding of the reasons why decisions are taken and the thinking that went into the decisions. Some lobbyists claim particular links with one political party or another, and this can be useful when that party is in government. When that party is, however, removed from office by the electorate, the affiliation may seem less worthwhile. A good lobbyist should be able to use the political understanding gained and apply that understanding to the situation of the time.

This chapter will explore the art of lobbying in the UK, EU and in the international context. It will highlight the predominant institutions that the lobbyist has to work with and influence and also explain how lobbying should be conducted.

WHY LOBBY?

In the first instance, why should an organization look to lobby? What benefits can it bring? For many organizations, these are fundamental questions. With resources being finite, one of the key drivers for a lobbyist is to be able to 'prove' the worth of lobbying in order to charge the organization for their services.

Lobbying can:

- Protect an organization – this can be from a number of sources such as a policy threat or a new regulation. Politicians also have a habit of reacting to the news agenda and will often 'name and shame' an organization or offer an unfavourable comment. Often such comments stem from a lack of understanding about the organization or the issue because the organization has failed to engage with the politician.
- Assist in identifying new opportunities – if an organization has not engaged with government then it is much less likely to be aware of policy developments that could be of benefit to it. Without this knowledge it will not be able to react and develop appropriate new products or services etc. You must consider that whilst you are not lobbying, your competitors will be and they will, therefore, gain an advantage.
- Help to build support – amongst politicians and civil servants, for instance for a policy position or new legislative development. The work of the disability rights organizations and charities was, for instance, used to great effect in persuading the new Labour Government to introduce the Disability Discrimination Act, which for the first time made discrimination against people with disabilities illegal.
- Raise a profile – lobbying can be used to make contact with those decision-makers who can impact on the activity of your organization. Such links can be especially useful when legislation is going through parliament and you wish to seek changes or when a new policy is being developed and you may be called upon to help provide information or advice in its formulation because of your pre-existing links.

Based on the above it can be said that there are several types of lobbying:

- bill lobbying – on legislation going through parliament;
- profile-raising lobbying – developing links with decision-makers;
- reactive lobbying – when something goes wrong.

Whichever type of lobbying your organization is engaged in there are a number of elements to a successful campaign. These elements form the basis of how lobbying should be conducted.

MONITORING

It is essential that a close watch is maintained on political proceedings. Traditionally this monitoring was confined to *Hansard*, which reproduces the previous day's proceedings from parliament, and future business. However, as government has grown and developed, this is now insufficient. Governments are now more adept at using electronic media, especially the internet, and make many of their announcements outside parliament. This means that any successful monitoring needs to think beyond just the strictly political.

Monitoring should also include audiences outside the immediate political arena. Often what these audiences say and the positions they adopt will influence the success of a lobbying campaign. These audiences will vary, depending on the nature of the campaign but consideration should be given to:

- trade bodies;
- trade unions;
- the media, especially trade publications;
- competitors.

Monitoring:

- provides opportunities for input into policymaking;
- allows a reaction to mentions of the organization in parliament, as this may have an impact on reputation;
- keeps you up to date with developments;
- allows the reaction of parliamentarians to the sector or organization to be tracked – if it is tending to be more unfavourable, then you can expect some unfavourable developments or policy coming forward;
- provides a record of the decisions taken by government.

It is imperative that early warning systems are established. Through a comprehensive monitoring system organizations can identify the policy or legislation that will affect them. The earlier this is spotted, the earlier its impact can be assessed and the earlier something can be done about it. This is especially important if the policy represents a threat to the organization.

Those delivering the monitoring effectively become the 'eyes and ears' of the organization in the institutions of government. Only once access to the information has been gained can any necessary lobbying take place.

Monitoring should include:

- Government websites – each government department (and Number 10 Downing Street) has its own website and these should be checked on a very regular basis. Look at the 'what's new' section of the site or the newsroom; this will take you to the latest information. However, some details can be 'hidden' on sites, such as on the pages that list current consultations. Make sure you sign up for e-mail lists as this often means that the information will be delivered direct to your PC. Yet, the internet and websites are not the be-all and end-all and should not be relied on totally.
- Media outlets – in each jurisdiction there will be particular media outlets that should be watched closely. In the United Kingdom, the *Today* programme (BBC Radio 4, 6–9am) is recognized as the start of the political day but also take care to read all the national daily newspapers. Be sure not to dismiss any, especially the tabloids. With government increasingly relying on the media to communicate with the general public, often policy will be trialled in the press giving a feel for potential future government policy and advance warning for those organizations involved. If a policy is trialled, seems to be popular and does not meet with a backlash then it may later appear on the statute book. It is, therefore, important that when this happens the organization knows its priorities and reacts accordingly. It should also be stressed that support as well as opposition to such policies can be communicated. As well as daily newspapers and the *Today* programme think about covering, for instance:
  - *New Statesman;*
  - *The Spectator;*
  - *Private Eye;*
  - *The Economist;*
  - *The House Magazine* (Westminster parliament);
  - *Holyrood* (Scottish parliament).
- Press releases – those issued by bodies, especially from government, often contain the real detail that you must master to enable an assessment of the potential impact. This is especially true of the large 'set

piece' events such as budgets or the Queen's Speech. For these events explanatory notes are often issued or, in the case of the Budget, the Red Book (Budget Pack) containing full details of the economic statistics upon which the government's decisions are based.

- Speeches – with the best will in the world the media only concentrates on very small sections and sound bites from speeches and this may not be the most important part as far as you are concerned. In addition, coverage is only given to the really important speeches, normally from the most high-profile members of government and, to a lesser extent, from the main opposition parties. Speeches should be looked at and the detail checked.
- Websites – include in your monitoring the websites of bodies involved in the wider policymaking community. These may include news sites, the sites of the political parties, third party organizations, and increasingly, blogs, etc.

Monitoring provides the raw materials upon which a successful lobbying campaign is based. Without knowledge of government thinking, how it has changed over time and what the current position is, the lobbying will not be successful.

For a consultant providing a client with a monitoring service, the aim is to prevent information overload. It is no longer that we do not know what goes in government but simply that there is so much information out there that it clouds the ability to make decisions and confuses the organization. Those providing a monitoring service will examine all the various sources of information, filter the information and then deliver it in a way that the client can look at and act upon. Inevitably the information has to be accompanied by advice about its impact and whether any action is required.

In parliamentary terms, monitoring needs to include:

- The Order Paper – contains information about the day's proceedings in the House of Commons including summary agenda and the order of business, future business, votes and proceedings, list of statutory instruments, Early Day Motions, questions for oral or written answer.
- Lords Minutes – contains information about the day's proceedings in the House of Lords including the agenda, notice of future business, minutes of proceedings and, because of the legal role that the House of Lords plays, judicial business.
- *Hansards* – for both the Commons and the Lords containing full information of all debates and answers to questions. A separate *Hansard* for standing committees (see below) is available.
- Weekly Agendas – for both the Commons and the Lords containing a full list of information such as select committee sessions.

As well as day to day events, special attention also needs to be paid to changes in political positions, such as in reshuffles. A watch needs to be maintained on changes in personnel at all levels in government. A change in cabinet or amongst ministers is known as a reshuffle and can take place either because the prime minister chooses to 'freshen up' his or her team or because a position becomes available (possibly through retirement or resignation). It is, however, imperative that a full monitoring service tracks personnel in all levels of government, the civil service, amongst committee memberships etc.

Lionel Zetter, Managing Director,
Parliamentary Monitoring Services Ltd

Without parliamentary monitoring, political news and political intelligence no public affairs campaign can hope to succeed.

Whether your campaign is designed to raise your profile, protect your reputation, or change the law it will undoubtedly fail unless you know how the issues are viewed by politicians. You also need to know – right from the outset of any campaign – who is on your side and (equally important) who is going to be opposing you.

The best provider will offer state of the art technology – combined with people possessing the political skills and experience to interpret the monitoring and provide the political intelligence.

WHAT DO YOU WANT TO DO?

Through the monitoring of the political system, media outlets and so on it has to be decided how to use the information. This can only be done if some clear objectives have been set. Every organization needs to understand:

- what its priority issues are – these should be related to their core operation;
- what it wants to achieve – these may be very commercial objectives for a company.

Some typical objectives may be:

- to maintain a stable regulatory environment;
- to ensure a level playing field;
- to allow greater access to markets;
- to communicate the core values of the organization;

- to communicate the commercial implications of government policy;
- to secure funds from government.

One of the best ways of finding out what the objectives for the organization are is to conduct a risk analysis session, sometimes called a SWOT session (strengths, weaknesses, opportunities, threats). This session should include key people from the organization, preferably from a senior level, to ensure that all parts of the organization have an opportunity in the objective setting process. It is also useful to include external advisors in such sessions. To exclude a part of the organization can lead to problems further down the line. The session should seek to:

- examine the current situation facing the organization;
- identify key issues;
- define the objectives for the organization going forward;
- develop the case to be delivered;
- decide on a strategy for implementation;
- assess the stakeholders involved;[2]
- consider solutions if problems are identified in government policy;
- establish the key messages that need to be delivered and how the organization should communicate these to its various audiences;
- decide on a timetable of activity and the level of resources required.

This session will obviously help set the priorities when monitoring. There are many issues to track. Which are the important ones for the organization? Which ones should just be tracked? Which ones require a reaction? This makes monitoring a more manageable task.

HOW POLICY IS MADE IN THE UK

Now that the issues upon which the organization wishes to lobby have been agreed, it is imperative that a complete understanding of how policy is made and decisions are taken on such matters is formed. No two policies are the same and the actors involved will vary but consider how policy is made by the UK government as a starting point.

The main players are described below.

Number 10 Downing Street

There has been much written about the centralization of power in the hands of the prime minister. This centralization has been taking place since the 1960s at the very least. Harold Wilson's creation of a 'kitchen cabinet' in effect brought more power into his hands, and those of his close advisers, away from the democratically elected politicians and the Cabinet. Every prime minister since that time has further developed his or her own power. Tony Blair has a Policy Directorate that normally consists of around 15 advisers, each with their own area of responsibility, and this is at the heart of policymaking. Advisers are political appointees and whilst they are each generally expert in their area, they also often have a political understanding. They will, therefore, be able to assess the political implications of a policy (this can mean damage or potential damage to the government or the prime minister). Be sure to identify the senior policy adviser with responsibility for the issue.

Formally, the role of the Policy Directorate is to:

- work with colleagues inside government, and policy specialists outside, to develop new ideas;
- prepare policy advice for the prime minister;
- ensure that the prime minister's decisions and views are fully carried out.

The advisers in the Policy Directorate are close to the prime minister and are, therefore, a good conduit to him. Advisers in the directorate also work closely with special advisers and can be useful when lobbying government departments. Having the authority of the prime minister behind them can really help their power to influence others!

The directorate also includes a number of foreign policy advisers and an appointments unit that advises the prime minister on a range of appointments, including Crown appointments.

As things stand, the prime minister has a chief of staff who has direct responsibility for leading and coordinating operations across Number 10. The Prime Minister's Office includes the:

- Communications and Strategy Unit – which includes three main units:
  - press office – deals with the media;
  - strategic communications unit – deals with longer term announcements;
  - research and information unit – provides information to Number 10.

  The Prime Minister's official spokesperson is part of the Communications and Strategy Unit, as is the Corporate Communications Unit and Direct Communications Unit.
- Government Relations Secretariat – deals with relations between Number 10 and the Labour Party but also the wider general public.

In addition it arranges the prime minister's visits as well as receptions and events held at Number 10.
- Policy Directorate – as described previously.

In addition, the Prime Minister's Office also contains a number of key individuals including:

- Deputy Chief of Staff;
- Principal Private Secretary;
- Director of Communications;
- Director of Events, Visits and Scheduling;
- Director of Political Operations;
- Head of Policy Directorate;
- Chief Adviser on Strategy;
- Director of Government Relations;
- Adviser of EU Affairs and Head of the European Secretariat;
- Adviser of Foreign Affairs and Head of the Overseas and Defence Secretariat;
- Parliamentary Private Secretary.

It is important to maintain a watch of the structure of 10 Downing Street as it does change, especially between prime ministers all of whom have their own ideas about how their inner sanctum should be run. Both the *Civil Service Yearbook* and *Dod's Civil Service Companion* are good ways of checking the current structure of Number 10.

- Cabinet committees – the Cabinet is the team that runs government business. In the past the prime minister was said to be *prima inter paris* (first among equals) among his or her cabinet colleagues but over the years has become more important. There are a number of reasons for this including the spotlight that the media places on the PM but it has led to accusations of presidential behaviour. The Cabinet, undoubtedly, still plays a role as it contains all ministers. The Cabinet also has a number of committees that bring together ministers, from senior and junior levels, who are relevant to the issue to enable them to discuss it in more detail. The Cabinet does not have enough time to discuss and decide on all the issues of the day so more emphasis has been placed on the role that these committees can play. They are also supported by a number of ministerial committees but the key is that all decisions that are made are binding on the full Cabinet. Often more controversial topics are dealt with by committees and they have helped to foster the sense of cross-departmental thinking.

  Examples of recent Cabinet committees include:

- Economic Development;
- External Relations and Defence.

Examples of recent ministerial committees include:

- Animal Rights Activists;
- Public Service Reform.

Government departments

Each department is made up of a series of people who you must include as part of your campaign. The most obvious starting point is with the relevant civil servants. Whilst much policy is initiated from 10 Downing Street it remains the case that the civil service builds and develops the policy and, in the case of parliamentary legislation, writes the bill. The civil service remains the heart of how policies are built up and developed. They draft the policies and are responsible for thinking through how they will be implemented. Any organization should get to know who its civil service contacts are. With many policies cutting across departments, it may be that the civil servants you need to contact are from a number of departments. However, civil servants are often placed under considerable pressure to complete policy and may not be aware of all its implications; this is especially the case as many do not have a commercial background. In this way organizations can assist in the policymaking process by offering expert advice that many civil servants are willing to consider.

Do not think that all lobbying has to be overtly political; civil servants still have a great deal of sway in dealing with issues such as procurement, distributing government funding, and contracting. They also retain a large say in how departmental policies are set within the broader outline of government policy. The civil service remains charged with implementing government policy.

Authority no longer resides solely in government departments. Since the 1980s, parts of the civil service have been moved into Executive Agencies that are meant to reflect more accurately the ethos of the private sector. In addition, there has been a substantial rise in the role of regulation and of the Regulators, again since the 1980s and the roll-out of privatization. It is more accurate to think of government as now covering:

- departments – each having some autonomy over its areas of policy;
- regulatory bodies – which exist to keep a watch on specialist sectors and the companies within them, eg the Financial Services Authority (FSA), Ofcom, Ofgem, Office of Fair Trading, Competition Commission;
- agencies – often charged with carrying out the commercial parts of government business, eg the Passport Agency;

- non-departmental public bodies (NDPBs) – issues that need to be moved away from the day to day control of a department are given to a NDPB, eg Health Education Authority, Countryside Commission;
- quasi-judicial bodies – established where the remit appears to fall between the department and the courts, eg the Advisory Conciliation and Arbitration Service, Local Government Commission.

Aside from the civil servants in each department, there are obviously the politicians. The very fact that they have reached a position of secretary of state, minister or junior minister means that they wield some power and influence over policy. Each department has a number of ministers and they each have their own areas of responsibility, those policy areas for which they speak on behalf of the government. Each department is headed up by a secretary of state (or in the case of HM Treasury, the Chancellor of the Exchequer) and they have overall responsibility for the running of the department and all its areas of responsibility. Just as the prime minister has advisers, each secretary of state has a number of special advisers. Again, these special advisers are political appointees and assist in the creation and delivery of policy as well as being the political 'eyes and ears' for the secretary of state. The role of special advisers has been somewhat controversial but they are now a well-established part of government. If you are dealing with more junior ministers do not assume that they do not have advisers. Sometimes these may be formal or informal.

You must make contact with the relevant minister as well as the secretary of state and be sure to establish contact with special advisers if you wish to have any hope of making your position known. The secretary of state will often receive a great deal of advice from their special advisers. Ministers are, at the end of the day, that part of each government department that is accountable to parliament. Whilst they do not tend to make policy without reference to others, the secretary of state and ministers, more generally, need to be kept informed of developments especially if there is likely to be media-generated interest. It has to be borne in mind though that most letters and papers sent to ministers never arrive with them; they are instead sent by their private office to the officials dealing with the matter for a response. It is only if you secure a meeting that you are really guaranteed a chance to put your argument to the minister.

Unfortunately, civil servants sometimes do not wish to hear comments or feedback on their policy for a number of reasons. Do not take this to mean that your comments are not correct or have no place in the development of the policy. This is why contact with those at a political level can be very important. Very often politicians and advisers will have an eye on the electoral and media implications of a policy so do not rely solely on the civil servants. You must, however, initiate contact with the civil servants as any minister contacted will inevitably insist that this contact has happened before they get involved.

Parliament

This audience includes not only backbench MPs from across all the parties but also the front bench spokespersons from the main opposition parties, the Conservatives and the Liberal Democrats. Their spokespersons largely shadow the government departments and have a shadow secretary of state in charge of their teams. There are also occasions when they are arranged as an opposition would like government to be, eg 'Homeland Security'. Also included in this parliamentary audience should be those who have shown a distinct interest or have a relevant 'responsibility'. Be sure to include:

- Those with a background in the area – they may have worked in an industry or have expressed an interest in it, possibly through previous parliamentary activity such as Parliamentary Questions or having sponsored or signed an Early Day Motion (EDM).[3]
- Members of relevant select committees[4] – select committees are one of the few parts of parliament that retain some real power and continue to act as a check on government. Some of the committees are, however, more important and powerful than others, eg the Treasury, Trade and Industry, Public Accounts and Transport. This power is often enhanced by the capabilities of the committee's members and, most importantly, its chair. The committees can choose their own topics for inquiry and this makes the role of the chair more important still. Some committee sessions are covered in the media and are often broadcast. This helps to give the topic concerned a higher profile. Each committee will also engage a number of specialists on its topic of inquiry. For those looking to contribute to the outcome of the inquiry then it is important that these advisers do not start from one particular perspective as this could influence the committee's final outcome. Part of a comprehensive monitoring programme should include press releases from select committees.
- Members of relevant All Party Groups[5] – in reality these groups are often run by interest groups or lobby groups. A useful option for an organization wishing to gain supporters in parliament may be to launch an All Party Group. Many of the groups are becoming more sophisticated in their approach and, for instance, the All Party Football Group have their own website and hold their own inquiries. These take evidence from interested groups, and then issue a report, much like a select committee. Although it does not have the formal powers of a select committee and the government is under no obligation to reply to a report, the All Party Group can use the inquiry to gain media coverage and raise the profile of the issue. A presentation to an All Party Group can be very useful, as would having them take up your

case. Part of a comprehensive monitoring programme should include press releases from All Party Groups and the list that is produced each week of forthcoming All Party Groups meetings.

- Backbench Groups – formal groups of MPs in each party can come together to campaign for a common set of policies or reflect a certain ideology. This is less fashionable in today's style of politics but groups such as the Campaign Group or the Tribune Group have been important in the Labour Party, and the Bow Group in the Conservative Party. Such groups can be considered slightly old-fashioned and their members are often considered to be fringe players but they are considered. More modern is the launching of a new think tank that can often attract wider groups of supporters and finance to a cause. The two major groupings of backbench MPs are the 1922 Committee for the Conservative Party and the Parliamentary Labour Party (PLP) for Labour, which are often addressed directly by the party leader.
- Backbench Committees – the Labour and Conservative parties have groups of MPs that come together to shadow the major departments of government. These groups are meant to discuss relevant policy and 'transmit' backbench feeling to the party leadership.
- Specialist 'groups' – need to be followed as groupings can spring up around particular issues or around pieces of legislation, for instance an informal group of Labour MPs emerged to campaign against tuition fees for students' higher education.

It is important that a careful watch is maintained on rising stars in all of the parties. This means checking the progress of MPs – look at who writes the speeches for leaders at party conferences, who researches the questions and answers for Prime Minister's Question Time etc.

One of the main sources of parliamentary support for a cause can be the constituency MP of the organization. This makes it imperative that the organization gets to know its MP. The MP may be able to provide advice on tactics to be adopted and may also be willing to take up your concerns. It may be that the MP may hold a position to assist directly with the issue or may have parliamentary contacts that can assist with the matter. The building of a network of parliamentary contacts is an important part of any communications programme. Your MP may lead a delegation to a minister and this can prove to be a valuable route to make your argument at the highest level. A minister may feel more comfortable taking representation on your behalf from an MP rather than directly from you. At general election times, actions such as meeting the candidates may be a useful activity but be sure not to be 'used' by one side or another; undertake meetings on your terms where possible.

Contact with a constituency MP may mean that the organization is asked to get involved in local activities, such as taking a table at a fundraising event. This may be appropriate but it has to be remembered that such payments can be considered as donations under the terms of the Political Parties, Elections and Referendums Act (PPERA) and the organization will be listed as having donated to the party. Again, this may be appropriate but the organization will have to consider balancing its political donations between all the parties otherwise there may be consequences with regard to reputation. The media or a competitor may use the listing to show that a donation has been made and try to cast aspersions.

MPs fulfil a number of roles, they:

- represent their constituents;
- keep a check on the executive;
- scrutinize and debate legislation;
- create legislation (occasionally).

MPs know how to highlight issues both in parliament and in the media and it is, therefore, important that they are taken seriously and kept informed. Even governments with very large majorities can use the 'will' of parliament as a handy excuse to amend or introduce legislation.

Each MP tends to have a PA/researcher in his or her Westminster office and another in the constituency. Some often have several but this depends on workload and resources. There are several MPs who also take on students to help them. Often the MPs' staff will also act as speechwriters, although some may employ a specialist writer. All these contacts can be useful not only as sources of information but also conduits to the MP. Contact should be maintained with the staff of MPs. Working as a researcher to an MP has often been viewed as a useful stepping stone into other jobs and professions, especially lobbying, because of a researcher's knowledge of parliament and how it operates.

Other sources

There are several other sources of policy in the UK. Each of the political parties has its own policy teams. The way in which policy is made in each of the parties varies, with the Liberal Democrats and Labour claiming to be the most democratic as they assign formal roles to their members in the decision-making processes, whereas the Conservative Party, even following recent reforms, has a more centralized process. Each of the parties has a head of policy and a supporting team made up of advisers specialising in particular areas. Another main source is think tanks, which are discussed in more detail in Chapter 4. Think tanks regularly produce reports, some of which are picked up by the political parties and turned into policy.

POLICY

Although, as discussed above, much policy is created amongst advisers, Number 10 and the wider policy community, there remain a number of processes through which the idea goes before it is enacted by parliament and becomes a law. Understanding this process is a key aspect of lobbying, because given the limited amount of parliamentary time available, the right option may not be legislation but a change in regulation, additional resources, revised guidance etc.

Consultations

The government undertakes more consultations now than at any time before. The 1997 Labour Government came to power promising more open and inclusive government and one of the ways in which it has attempted to demonstrate this commitment has been to consult more widely. There is now, in addition, guidance to government departments on how to conduct consultations, their form, length and so on. It has to be remembered, however, that this is only guidance and can be ignored!

More consultations are also taking place across government departments. 'Joined-up' thinking is encouraged and as issues become generally more complex more than one department is often involved. One department though remains predominant – HM Treasury. Before any legislation is progressed, the issue will have been consulted on in government but HM Treasury will have to have been convinced of its merits.

Traditionally government consultations take place in the form of Green and White papers. Green papers outline policy options being considered by government and can be debated in parliament or examined by select committees. White papers outline a proposed government policy and request comments. Responses are now more often made available and put on the departmental website.

Alongside Green and White papers, departments are now making more use of general consultation papers on major items of policy. These are Green Paper in nature, outlining the position and options, but with a White tinge, ie being quite firm in preferring a particular policy option.

Again, a further form of consultation that is being adopted is for the government to issue a draft bill and for a parliamentary committee to be established that examines it in more detail before a version of the bill is introduced formally into parliament for scrutiny. Examples of this include the Communications Bill and the Financial Services and Markets Bill.

From a lobbying perspective it is recommended that you are involved in the process as early as possible. If a Green Paper is issued then ideally a submission should be made. It is more difficult to suggest changes to policy further down the line, especially if you have not been involved in the earlier stages.

Once the policy has been consulted on, it is passed to the specialist draftsman and a 'bill team' is established in the relevant department that is charged with overseeing the bill, and possible changes through its parliamentary process. If you are lobbying on a bill then you need to know who heads the team and make contact with them to make your points to them.

The bill then enters parliament.

The parliamentary process

If you are lobbying on a piece of primary legislation, a bill, it is important to know what type of bill you are dealing with. The vast majority of bills are government bills. There are, however, three other types:

- private member's bills;
- private bills;
- hybrid bills.

The majority of government bills are outlined at the start of each parliamentary session in the Queen's Speech. This outlines the government's legislative priorities for the year but bills can be introduced that are not in the Queen's Speech. The Queen's Speech usually consists of around 15–20 bills. These can be formally introduced in the House of Commons or the House of Lords.

There are many books that detail in some considerable depth how legislation proceeds through parliament.[6] A clear understanding of the legislative process is a prerequisite for any lobbyist. In a simplified form, the full legislative process can be said to be:

- First Reading – formal introduction into parliament.
- Second Reading – first stage of real debate on the floor of the House where your points may be raised. No amendments can be made at this point but it is important that you have begun the process of briefing parliamentarians.
- Committee Stage – in the Commons a standing committee of around 18–25 MPs along the same party lines as the House looks in detail at the bill. The committee's membership often reflects those with an interest or understanding of the issues involved. Amendments can be moved and passed by any member although given the governmental majority it is unlikely any change of which they do not approve will go through. In the Lords, this stage is taken by a Committee of the

Whole House. Rather than individual MPs being selected, any peer can take part and move amendments, although by convention votes on amendments are not usually taken at this stage. The key difference is that in the Lords, the government does not always have a majority. This can be crucial in lobbying terms.

- Report (or Consideration) Stage – all members of the House look at the bill in more detail as it has been amended in committee. New amendments and clauses can be introduced at this stage. However, it is more difficult to introduce at this stage than in the previous Committee Stage. Votes are taken at this stage and changes can be made to bills but to do this lobbyists need to have fully briefed parliamentarians and prepared the ground in the early stages. A number of more external factors may also come into play such as what time the vote takes place. In the House of Lords, if your amendment is scheduled later in the evening then your chances of defeating the government are lessened as there are fewer peers around.
- Third Reading – this can sometimes take place immediately after Report Stage, and represents the final agreement of the bill. In the Commons amendments cannot be introduced at this stage whereas in the Lords they can. Third Reading is, under normal circumstances, short, but this can change if a bill is very controversial. If this is the case then parliamentarians will look for every opportunity to make the most of the parliamentary time available. Also, do not forget that a bill has to be passed successfully by both the Commons and the Lords so once one House has passed it, it moves to the other. The agreement of both Houses is required. The will of the elected chamber, the Commons, will usually prevail but that does not stop some disagreements taking place. The two Houses will sometimes play 'ping pong' with a bill until agreement is reached. Only under very exceptional circumstances will the Commons impose its will on the Lords through the use of the Parliament Act 1949.
- Royal Assent – finally, when both Houses have agreed the bill it is sent for Royal Assent. When this has been given the bill becomes an act.

It is increasingly common that much of the detail of an act is agreed through regulation. These regulations are passed through the introduction of statutory instruments (SIs) in parliament. A lobbyist needs to be vigilant about the introduction and passing of SIs as often these can have more impact than the contents of an act and lobbying can also take place on them.

Private member's bills are introduced by backbench parliamentarians; the opportunity to introduce a private member's bill is their only opportunity to introduce their piece of legislation. The chances of success, however, remain very slim mainly because of the lack of time and, normally, the lack of government support and the majority that brings in the Commons. There are though examples of success such as Lord Clement-Jones' bill banning tobacco advertising that was successfully passed in 2002.

There are a number of ways in which members can introduce a bill. The majority come about by taking part in an annual ballot in the Commons to decide on who has priority. MPs enter the ballot, if they wish, and are given priority (1-20) in the order in which they are drawn. For lobbyists this is an important time. Although private member's bills are unlikely to succeed they can provide a platform to raise an issue in parliament and among the wider public, can generate interest or if the bill progresses into its Second Reading gain a commitment from government. Those who come higher up the list will gain more of a hearing in parliament and that is where lobbyists start and then work their way down. The MP will chose his or her own bill to introduce but may be influenced by the government that could want a bill introduced, personal interest in a topic or, most importantly for a lobbyist, the information or representations they receive from an outside organization.

A private member's bill can also be introduced as a ten-minute rule bill, for which slots in the parliamentary timetable are allocated on a 'first-come, first-served' basis.

The two other forms of bills, mentioned above, are private bills and hybrid bills. Private bills apply to certain bodies or organizations, not the general public, which other bills do. Unlike other bills these are introduced by the body seeking to make the change, not by a parliamentarian. Private bills were often used most in relation to major construction deals but this is no longer the case. Specialist parliamentary agents are often employed to deal with private bills as they are so specialist. A hybrid bill simply brings together elements of public and private bills.

For a lobbyist looking to raise the profile of an issue or attempting to gain information from ministers there are a number of clear paths of activity. All of these rely upon contact having been made with parliamentarians and having convinced them of the worth of your case. In terms of monitoring, this type of information should be being tracked as it may be that rival organizations or bodies are also working with parliamentarians and their work may not be in your best interests! Some of these paths of activity include:

- Ministerial statements – the Labour Government moved away from the practice of government policy statements being made through questions being 'planted' by its MPs, allowing for a new government policy to be announced. Instead it relies more heavily on formal ministerial statements in parliament and written statements. These statements allow ministers to bring forward policy in parliament whilst trying to maximize their impact. For a lobbyist it can be very important to get hold of these statements on the day that they are released, so building a good relationship with the parliamentary unit of each department can be useful. You will know that they are due to be made as they will be listed in that day's Order Paper. Try to get hold of the statement through the unit on the day of its release, if not then it will be available in the next day's *Hansard*.

- Oral questions – each day questions are asked in parliament with each government department taking its turn. MPs enter a ballot to establish the order in which questions are taken. Many more questions are, however, tabled than are answered in parliament with the remainder becoming written questions. The answers to the questions are prepared by civil servants in each department.
- Written questions – put down by parliamentarians to gain a response from the government department.
- Prime Minister's Question Time – the big set piece political event of the week where not only MPs but also the opposition leaders get their chance to 'grill' the prime minister. PMQs have changed in nature in recent years and the PM is now usually much more fully briefed on the answers to give. A further change has been the rise in friendly questions that allow the PM to show how much his or her government has done on a certain topic. Such sycophantic questions are increasingly common. PMQs is guaranteed media coverage and the chamber is always packed with MPs. This can make it very useful if an MP asks a question of relevance to you and especially if one of the leaders of the opposition parties takes up your cause. Unlike backbench MPs who simply ask one question, the opposition leaders get to pose several and can develop an argument during the course of questioning.
- Adjournment debates – as well as taking part in debates on bills, as discussed above, a further way to raise your issue can be through adjournment debates. Once again, MPs have to enter a ballot to have the chance of initiating a debate. If successful, the MP can start a debate on any topic. They will introduce the debate, which increasingly take place in Westminster Hall, and a minister has to respond. Depending on the topic, other MPs may also take part.
- EDMs – mentioned above, can be encouraged through lobbying. If successful in encouraging an MP to put down an EDM then the next task is to secure a high number of signatories. Only if a large number of MPs sign the statement can you 'prove' its worth.
- Opposition debates – the opposition is assigned a set number of days in the parliamentary calendar in which it can raise its own debates. These debates usually make the most of the opportunity to raise issues of current public interest, eg the economy, the health service.

The House of Lords also has oral and written questions and adjournment debates. It is important that those lobbying do not denigrate the role that the House of Lords can play in raising an issue and in obtaining information. Often the level of debate is 'higher' in the House of Lords, for instance, longer amounts of time allocated to adjournment debates. Debates also often benefit from the level of expertise in the House of Lords.

Along with the Queen's Speech, the Budget is the other big set piece parliamentary event of the year. The Budget takes place in March each year but this varies in an election year if a new government enters office. The Budget sets out the government's financial strategy and also provides the economic statistics that demonstrate whether its economic policies are having the impact expected. The Budget contains information about taxation and spending. However, a lesser rival on the political scene is the 'Pre-Budget Report' (or 'Green Budget'), which takes place the previous November. The real worth of this has been challenged by some but one thing is certain, it enables the government to raise its economic profile twice a year. To those less sceptical, it provides an opportunity to comment on and feedback to government on their budgetary plans.

The Budget is not set in stone from day one and again is open to lobbying. There is a large degree of political input in decisions about priorities and spending but it remains up to HM Treasury and its various advisers, economists and statisticians about how this shapes up into a Budget. Option papers are drawn up by bodies such as HM Treasury and other government bodies in this area such as HM Customs & Revenue (HMCR). Those interested in helping to shape the tax and spend policies of government will want to be involved as early as possible in the development of the Budget. Those bodies seeking to influence the government's financial strategy, economic policy, encourage taxation or tax relief, or spending will want to be involved. The whole Budget process and its influence on the operation of government and its policies demonstrate the role and power of HM Treasury.

HM Treasury also controls the Comprehensive Spending Review, which allocates monies to individual departments and programmes for a three-year period. This typically takes place every two years and is a further control that HM Treasury exerts.

The Budget is debated in both Houses of Parliament and the budgetary measures proposed by the Chancellor are published as the Finance Bill. The government can expect to receive criticism during the debate but does not expect to be defeated on any reading votes. This is the one real piece of legislation that the government *knows* it will pass. Amendments can be proposed and made to the Finance Bill by the Commons but not by the Lords.

If your issue involves tax or spending, what is the position of HM Treasury? Timing is important when deciding upon which political audience to contact about your issue. Generally speaking, your first port of call should be the government and its advisers. Or, if you think that making the issue too political early on could be detrimental to your case, contact backbench government MPs or those known to have a good enough relationship with the relevant minister to try to exert an influence on the policy.

It has to be recognized that as soon you engage with any of the opposition, the issue may become a very political one and this may, in turn, give it a much higher profile in parliament or even among the general public if the media become involved.

For this reason, it may not be right to make it a political issue straight away. If, however, the government is showing little sign of making movement on the issue or it digs its heels in and refuses to listen to your position, then the opposition may have a very valuable role to play. For instance, if a bill is already proceeding through parliament and it is going through the House of Lords then the best chance of influencing the legislation may be through working with the opposition parties.

HOW TO LOBBY

The first stage of the programme is to understand the political environment in which you are operating. Obviously, as described above, this means knowing your way around the political and government institutions you need to influence. Yet you also need to know the politics and this can vary day to day. This is obviously not an area that can be explained in a text but instead comes with experience.

Once you have all this, you are ready to start to consider your lobbying strategy. In essence, you are making contact with those who are making or who can influence an outcome or decision. When writing a lobbying strategy, think about:

- The environment – what is the change you are looking to make, what are the current policies, has anything been said about your issue?
- Whereabouts in the system is the policy – is it still with civil servants, is it in consultation? Knowing where it is in the system will help you to decide with whom you need to engage.
- The outcome – what are you aiming to achieve?
- The people – who in government or in the wider policymaking setting do you need to contact – ministers, advisers, backbench MPs, civil servants?
- The approach – how will you convince them that a change is needed, what do you need to be able to prove your case, what is your

justification, do you need to undertake activity that increases the political pressure on them?
- The messages – what are you saying?
- Your allies – are there others of a similar mind who may offer support to your cause?[7]
- The media – can you develop the campaign?[8]
- Overall – what about the timescales you are working to, are there events that need to be considered?
- Always be sure to consider the potential aftermath of your campaign.

You may often have to present the strategy to others in your organization or to your client, or potential client. Think about their demands and where they will need to see activity taking place. Be sure to explain why each action is necessary and what benefits it may bring. Never take for granted that your audience for this type of presentation knows anything about lobbying and always be sure to explain every element of your strategy. In some instances, you may also need to turn the strategy into a proposal or into a board report. Again, understand the audience you are writing for and you will not go far wrong.

Overall, the key point to consider with any strategy is that it needs to be flexible. If the environment changes then the lobbying strategy needs to be altered.

CONTACT PROGRAMME

Establishing contact with the policymakers is the heart of the lobbying campaign. Once you have identified the right people then decide how you approach them. This is usually done through a briefing paper accompanied by a covering letter. A briefing paper should be no longer than two or two-and-a-half sides of A4 and should:

- introduce the issue;
- describe the organization;
- set out the nature of the problems;
- suggest a solution;
- provide contact details for further details.

Suggesting a solution as part of a briefing paper is essential. There are only a very limited number of occasions when not presenting a solution to the problem is acceptable. The solution may be a revised clause in a parliamentary bill, suggestions for new legislation, or a regulation. Highlighting an issue without proposing an answer will not lead to successful lobbying. The briefing paper has to be appropriate for the audience being approached and has to appeal and be relevant to them. Civil servants will expect more detail of a technical nature whilst with MPs it is appropriate to concentrate a little more on the main thrust of your argument. Do not be afraid to use language that may appeal to your audience and try to hit a 'raw nerve' if possible.

The briefing paper has to convince its recipient of the merits of your case so try to bring as much evidence to bear as possible. Look for existing research or comment, or maybe consider commissioning your own. Make liberal use of past comments by government, parliamentary debates, select committee recommendations etc. Part of the battle in building an argument is identifying its holes and missing elements and addressing these before someone else has the opportunity to fatally undermine your case. When writing the briefing paper keep asking the question 'so what?' This will help to focus you and strengthen the paper.

Again when researching your argument look to build it through:

- a parliamentary search;
- a web search – increasingly useful, especially as more backdated *Hansard* become available;
- printed materials – should not be ignored, ask yourself what the party's last general election manifesto said about your issue.

As a more general point, you should never hesitate to make the most of the various databases and publications that are available. There are often several versions of these available from different publishers or producers. Shop around for the best deal and make sure the version you take is the right one for you. Resources are always limited so before making any decision, see if a free trial is available. You may wish to consider:

- Biographies – *Dod's Parliamentary Companion* has always been the traditional source of biographical information on MPs and peers. It is also available online. Away from these official biographies, some additional colour and insight is provided by the profile books by Andrew Roth and Byron Criddle. These are also very interesting to read!
- Press[9] – numerous databases exist that give access to past press articles. Also, do not forget that what the press will write about in the future is also of great importance.
- Website checks – increasingly technology is allowing for websites to be checked by dedicated software. Companies exist that will provide a close check of any changes made to websites, eg press releases, consultations etc.
- The civil service – the *Civil Service Yearbook* provides details of the position, titles and so on of civil servants. Dod's also provides a similar service that includes some biographical information.

- PMS – the PMS Parliamentary Guide provides contact details for departments and office of Ministers and MPs, helping you in your contact programmes. It also covers Westminster, Scotland, Wales and Europe.
- Register of Members Interests – to provide you with full details of the current income from outside sources for MPs and other donations/ gifts accepted.
- Electoral Commission – the commission's website contains details of all political donors, which can be useful!
- Free services – subscribe to news alerts that provide details of political activity. These should not be your sole source of information but are a useful 'double check'.

The covering letter, which accompanies the briefing paper, should be signed by someone senior in the organization and should always be sent to a named individual. This will show how importantly the issue is being treated by you but also demonstrates to the opinion former that they are being dealt with by a senior member of your organization. The letter should also be tailored to reflect the position of the recipient and why you are writing to them in particular. For an MP this may include a reference to their background or a reference from *Hansard*. It is imperative that all names and titles are spelt correctly and that if you list a position, that it is correct. On some issues you may need to write to many parliamentarians, especially if lobbying on a piece of legislation, but tailoring each letter remains essential. Circulars can be spotted and often end up in the waste bin!

In both the briefing paper and the covering letter you need to be very clear about the issue you are raising – what it is, why it is important and what the solution is. Bear this in mind in all contact, at whatever level.

In the letter be clear about what you are asking for or seeking. Very often the best way to communicate your position fully is through a one-to-one meeting. In these circumstances, the briefing paper is used to highlight your concerns, filling in more detail and answering any questions that the policymaker may have. The briefing paper will help the policymaker to decide whether or not to meet.

Once the letter and briefing paper have been sent then follow them with a call to the office to ensure receipt. If a meeting is being sought then try to secure it when speaking to the office. Policymakers will rarely respond themselves to the letter and briefing paper, it is up to you to chase them! Keep accurate records of dates of contact with offices; note the names and numbers of those you speak to and the nature of the conversation. This will help if you have to call back at a later date.

If a meeting is secured then try to ensure flexibility on dates – policy-makers are inevitably very busy people, especially if they are advisers.

Try to accommodate their requests and not be too elusive with your own availability.

- Those attending the meeting should be of a senior level when dealing with MPs or government, whereas for a civil service meeting they will appreciate those with a firm grasp of the detail. In the UK it is not appropriate for outside lobbyists to attend a meeting on their own but you can take them along with you. You are always the best advocate of your position and will be taken more seriously by those you are meeting; they prefer to hear it direct from the 'horse's mouth'.

During a meeting take notes so that you have an accurate record of the event. This will help to ensure that if any actions are agreed they are followed up and to provide an accurate record of the discussions and issues covered.

After the meeting has taken place it is good practice to write a 'thank you' letter and provide any information that was promised. It can also be a useful reminder to the policymaker you met – perhaps they agreed to some actions that can be referred to in the letter.

Contact programmes do not only have to be engaged in when an organization has a problem, they can also be used to raise your profile. The aim of this type of contact building would be to ensure that if government or the civil service is looking at policy development then you would be involved. The input of outside bodies is often welcomed by those making policy as it helps to ensure that the policy is workable, what the reaction to it will be and to iron out any faults that there may be.

There are a number of events that you may wish to consider as part of a contact programme:

- Dinner with a group of parliamentarians – ideally these should be one-party events to avoid the possibility of turning it into a party political event. If the MPs are expert in an area or have been known to the organization for some time then a cross-party event may be more appropriate.
- A parliamentary reception – preferably this should take place in or around Westminster for the UK Parliament, Holyrood for the Scottish Parliament or Cardiff Bay for the Welsh Assembly. Politicians do not like to move very far from the parliament for a number of reasons including the possibility of being called back for votes. If you are holding a reception further away then transport should be offered. In previous years, receptions were used as glorified opportunities to entertain parliamentarians. Now, however, the emphasis is on events with a more specific purpose, preferably a policy outcome. This makes

an event of more use to senior executives within your organization but also to the parliamentarians who may wish to attend.
- A parliamentary exhibition – an MP, possibly your constituency MP, enters a ballot to be allocated a slot to enable them to hold an exhibition, usually in the Upper Waiting Gallery. Such exhibitions can prove a useful way to raise profile amongst parliamentarians and also the media, all of whom use that area and pass by. The exhibition needs to be exciting and informative.

Each of these activities have their own 'dos and don'ts' but a general set of principles would be:

- provide parliamentarians with plenty of notice;
- be prepared that parliamentary activity may take precedence over your event – even with the best organization in the world, parliamentary business can arise at the last minute and interrupt your event;
- be sure to organize them at a time that does not interfere with parliamentary business;
- do not organize an event on a Friday, this is the constituency day for MPs so they will not be around Westminster (also bear in mind that they often leave London on Thursday evening);
- never let an event overrun, be sure to make it comfortable for parliamentarians to leave the event;
- after the event always write to thank the participants; you can also use this opportunity to summarize any arguments, follow up on promised activity or answer any questions that may have arisen.

Later chapters will examine ways in which you can encourage your chosen audience to believe that your issue is of importance and that they should take note. You should seek opportunities to raise the profile of your issue. This may be through the media, events organized around the issue, research into the issue, or party conference activity.[10]

Lord Bell, Chairman, Chime Communications plc.

It's important to remember that in a representative democracy all are entitled to have their opinion listened to and their views taken account of. The problem is how to make that happen and that's what public affairs is all about. Remember, if you want to win, you need people to support your point of view and make sure that the rules of the game don't work against you. It is perfectly possible to change intended legislation or to ensure amendments that protect your interest if your case is well-presented to the right people.

MEETINGS

When meeting with a politician it is essential that those doing the meeting are fully briefed about the person they are meeting. A pre-brief should be provided that includes:

- a suggested agenda – how the meeting should run;
- proposed questions to ask – this will help the meeting to follow and maximize the possibility of a favourable outcome;
- a clear indication of what you want from the meeting – this is crucial, if the aim of the meeting is not clear then there is no real reason to meet;
- a biography – utilize Dod's and Roth/Criddle.

For details about the person's past, their activity, prime concerns etc to inform the pre-brief then undertake:

- a search of parliamentary activity – what have they been doing and saying, whether they have been asking questions in a certain area or been active on a topic.
- a press search – to see what they have been saying in the press, very often at a local level, or what is being said about them;
- an internet search – this is especially useful for those meetings that are taking place with less high-profile politicians or civil servants.

When undertaking a meeting programme:

- Meet with the person leading the meeting beforehand to talk them through the pre-brief, to discuss the meeting, the person and what to do.
- Take notes during all meetings.
- Be sure to send a thank you that can note any agreements made and follow-up activity required by either party.
- Ensure that they are aware of the timings involved – ministers will rarely be in a position to give more than around 30 minutes of their time; MPs slightly longer, around 30–40 minutes.
- Manage the expectations of those conducting the meetings – it can happen that meetings are cancelled at short notice and that sometimes, MPs especially, fail to turn up for meetings. This is rare but it can happen.
- Keep in contact with the offices of those being met to confirm the meetings. When a meeting is initially set up a fax or e-mail should be sent that sets out the time, date and location of the meeting and those people from your side who will attend. A few days before the meeting, ring again to reconfirm arrangements.

In many ways the central part of any meeting programme is to be sure that contact is maintained over the next weeks, months and years. There is nothing worse for politicians than for contact to be made and then for them to hear from you only when there is a problem. To maintain a good relationship ensure that opportunities for ongoing contact are utilized – company results, new corporate social responsibility (CSR) activities, local events and so on. Similarly always look to extend your network of contacts, for instance a new appointee to a select committee, a promotion etc. In this way, when assistance is required, politicians will view your representations more favourably. General communications with parliamentarians can very often be useful, for instance some organizations may send out a regular newsletter to update their parliamentary contacts, some may send them to all parliamentarians across the Commons and the Lords. The parliamentarian should always be offered a way of contacting you – this may mean providing your contact details but you could also think about setting up a dedicated phone line for parliamentarians to call in case they need answers to questions or need feedback on a constituency matter.

If possible, maintain a contact database so that you can easily see:

- who has been met/contacted;
- when they were met/contacted;
- the issue they were contacted about;
- any follow-up actions required (and who is responsible for their delivery).

The cornerstone of any meeting programme should include:

- constituency MPs;
- the relevant minister;
- civil servants;
- special advisers in relevant department;
- the lead policy adviser, Number 10 Policy Directorate;
- key parliamentarians, such as chair of relevant select committee.

Once the contact has been made, the briefings undertaken and the arguments made, then you hope to achieve a favourable outcome. This outcome will obviously depend on why lobbying was engaged in the first instance. You may be looking to change the clause of a bill. In this case make sure you accurately monitor the bill, its debates and its amendments. Do not, however, forget that getting a statement or answer 'on the record' in *Hansard* can provide the clarification that you need; it can also prove useful legally. As a lobbyist you must be able to demonstrate the outcome of the campaign – whether you win or lose.

LOCAL GOVERNMENT

Whilst most of the 'big decisions' are taken at the UK or national parliaments, it is essential that the importance of local government is recognized. In this age where an increasing amount of policy is decided centrally but its implementation takes place at a local level, the role of local authority is increased.

Civil servants at local level are called officers and are also independent and non-political in the same way. They examine issues and make recommendations to the council. The decisions may be taken in committees, which reflect the political balance of the council, or by the politicians who run the council. Increasing numbers of councils now have a central cabinet with a councillor who has responsibility for an area of policy, in the same way that a secretary of state does in the UK government.

Local authorities have particular powers in planning and social services. There are really three levels of local government:

- county councils – a strategic role in the delivery of services such as education, social services, police, fire and waste;
- district, borough, and city councils – the emphasis is placed more on the implementation side on planning and development, environmental health, housing, refuse collection and leisure services;
- parish and town councils – largely historic levels of government with only limited powers, they do still maintain a consultation role in planning applications.

London, with its borough structure, in essence brings together all three of these levels into one.

Aside from its practical policy role and implementation of policy set centrally, local government also sets the levels of council tax to pay for these services. Central government tries to control this power and sets limits on spending and taxation increases but it remains a pivotal role locally. Most importantly, local government represents local people and this link to local opinion has to be recognized when any lobbying is being undertaken. For instance, in planning matters the requirements and needs of the local community have to be at the heart of any arguments. This is why it is important to gain the support of residents and local groups alongside councillors.[11]

Understand the dynamics of the council you are looking to influence. Some place the role of committees above all else; others prefer to hear from councillors, such as the relevant ward councillor; whilst others are largely controlled by the political group or by the leader of the council. Undertake an assessment before you start lobbying otherwise your arguments and points of contact may be misplaced.

The role of local government is also developing as it is encouraged to seek greater involvement of the private sector. Its other main challenge lies, therefore, in attracting investment to an area. There are other bodies involved in this process so do not look just at local government but also at, for instance, regional development agencies. In future, there may also be regional assemblies in parts of England.

SCOTLAND

The Scottish Parliament was established following a referendum held in 1997. The establishment of a parliament was a longstanding commitment of the Labour Party and the 'yes' vote was seen as an endorsement of the party's belief in the devolution of power. As with local government, the Labour Government has attempted to give more decision-making powers to local people through the parliament. The decision to make the electoral system a more proportional one than that enjoyed at Westminster elections was seen as further 'proof' of this commitment. So far, both governments in Scotland (following elections in 1999 and 2003) have been Labour and Liberal Democrat coalitions. The parliament has a number of areas over which it maintains control whilst others are 'reserved' for Westminster:

- devolved matters include health, education, training, local government, social work, housing, planning, tourism, prisons, legal, economic development, the police, environment, sports and arts;
- reserved matters include foreign policy, defence, national security, fiscal, economic, monetary system, constitutional matters, immigration and nationality.

Policymaking in Scotland is similar to that in Westminster and key influences include:

- First Minister – is the prime minister of Scotland and comes from the majority party in the parliament or, as so far has been the case, the largest party in the coalition government. As with the prime minister, the First Minister appoints ministers to form the Scottish Executive (the Scottish government). The First Minister has a number of advisers who will offer assistance in policy and media relations and are, therefore, a key influence on the direction of the government.
- Ministers – each minister in the Scottish Executive has responsibility for a portfolio. Each department has its own civil servants who operate in the same manner as their UK counterparts. Due to the government being a coalition, departments are allocated between the two parties,

and each also has a junior minister who comes from the other party. In this way the Scottish Executive is meant to reflect the political make-up of the coalition.

- Members of the Scottish Parliament (MSPs) – there are, in effect, two classes of MSP because of the electoral system. The system is based on a 'first-past-the-post' constituency element (whoever gains the most votes in the constituency wins) and then a regional element (Scotland is divided into five areas, each of which is given a number of seats; these are allocated to the parties on the basis of the vote gained in the area. Each party puts together a list of potential MSPs and these seats are given to the candidates on the list in order of priority, eg if Labour gains one additional seat in an area it is allocated to the person who tops their list). It is claimed that those MSPs voted into the parliament on the 'first-past-the-post' system have more legitimacy than the list MSPs because they are known to the electorate and campaign for their seat, whereas those on the list are simply selected by their parties and the electorate do not know them. This is quite a simplistic analysis as it takes no note of the personalities of those involved. Some quite high-profile MSPs are those from their party's 'list'. There is, however, some element of truth as it does colour the way in which MSPs view each other and how the media views them.
- The Scottish parliament has a number of committees that reflect the structure of the executive's departments. In the same way that a select committee will undertake inquiries, these committees also fulfil this role to ensure that the executive is held to account.
- Opposition – again, partly as a consequence of the electoral system but also of the way in which the media operates, parties with relatively small numbers of MSPs can exert an influence. The Opposition in Scotland currently includes the Conservative Party and Scottish National Party but can also be said to include the Scottish Socialist Party (SSP). The votes of these parties do not have a geographical quality so it is worth knowing if there is a 'favoured' party if you are lobbying in a particular area. All the main opposition parties have spokespersons who speak along departmental lines roughly mirroring those of the executive.

From the perspective of lobbying, it is important to consider:

- Is the matter a devolved one?
- If so, which Minister and department are responsible?
- Who are the relevant MSPs both for the constituency and for the area?

A lobbying campaign would then follow the same basic principles as those for Westminster lobbying. It should not be forgotten that there remains a position of Secretary of State for Scotland in the UK who has responsibility for ensuring that Scottish matters are not ignored in the UK.

WALES

The National Assembly for Wales was also voted into existence following a referendum in 1997. However, as its name implies being an assembly it has much less power and authority than its counterpart, a parliament, in Scotland.[12] This should not, however, be seen as a sign to ignore the assembly, because it plays an important role in Welsh politics and policy-making. The assembly took over the powers of the former Welsh Office, which operated out of Westminster and looked after Welsh matters. This means that the assembly has powers over secondary legislation (regulations) but not primary legislation (new acts). It has authority in areas such as economic development, culture, education, environment, health, local government etc.

Such regulations, the ways in which the laws passed by Westminster actually operate, can be crucial. The Welsh Assembly can debate any area of policy, including those controlled totally by Westminster, but can only create secondary legislation in the devolved matters.

In the two sets of elections to date (1999 and 2003), the Labour Party has formed the government but with only a minority of seats in the assembly in the first election, and a slim majority in the second.

Policymaking in Wales is similar to that in Westminster and key influences include:

- First Secretary – the leader of party in government with the power to select secretaries. The First Secretary has a number of advisers on policy and media matters.
- Secretaries – the equivalents of ministers, the Secretaries each have responsibility for a department that controls an area of policy. Each department has its own civil service.
- Members of the Welsh Assembly – Assembly Members (AMs) also have the same issues to contend with as their Scottish counterparts, their numbers, too, come from both constituencies and lists. The assembly has committees that shadow government departments and hold inquiries into relevant policy issues to help hold the government to account.
- Opposition – as Scotland has the SNP, Wales has Plaid Cymru (PC) and they too enjoy a high profile in their country. The Liberal Democrats

and the Conservatives are also currently in Opposition. All three have party spokespersons mirroring the governing Secretaries. The votes of these parties do not have a geographical quality so it is worth knowing if there is a 'favoured' party if you are lobbying in a particular area.

Once again, it should not be forgotten that there remains a position of Secretary of State for Wales in the UK who has responsibility for ensuring that Welsh matters are not ignored in the UK.

EUROPE

The European Union and lobbying its institutions deserves a whole book to itself. This section is meant as a brief overview rather than a detailed guide but it has to be remembered that the basics of lobbying remain the same. However, you need to bear in mind:

- the longer time scales involved in policymaking;
- the level of detailed argument required in lobbying as a consequence of the timescales;
- the role of member states and national lobbying.

The main institutions of the European Union are:

- The Commission – this is essentially the civil service of the Union and is divided into a number of Directorate-Generals (DGs) that have responsibility for a policy area, eg DG Trade, DG Enterprise, DG Employment and Social Affairs. Each DG is headed-up by a Commissioner who is a political appointment. Each of the EU Member State countries is allowed to nominate a Commissioner. Their portfolios are decided by the Commission President and agreed by the European Parliament. The president is himself a political appointment by the member states.
- Each Commissioner, when given a portfolio, appoints his or her own Cabinet that advises them on policy matters. As with domestic departments, some of the DGs enjoy a higher profile than others and, therefore, so does the Commissioner.
- The Parliament – the European Parliament consists of 732 Members (MEPs). The MEPs are elected by each member state, with the larger states being given more MEPs. As with parliaments the world over, it exists to scrutinize legislation and keep a check on the Executive (the Commission). The parliament also has a number of political groupings that generally reflect the left/right breakdown of the parties that are represented in the parliament. These groupings often act in unison on

issues and often have their own organization/leadership that act as support. If we take the example of the UK, each of the parties elected to the parliament have their own leader and support mechanisms.

- Council of Ministers – the Council consists of a number of councils, each covering a specific policy area. The representatives on each of the councils are the ministers from the member states that have responsibility for that policy area. The full Council is made up of the leaders from each of the member states. The presidency (leadership) of the full Council rotates every six months, with each member state taking it in turns to decide on the policy direction and priorities for its six-month term.
- Permanent Representation – each member state has a team of advisers and officials that formally act as a point of liaison between the national governments of the member state and the bodies of the European Union. The UK's Permanent Representation is known as UKREP.

From the perspective of those looking to influence the policies and decisions of the European Union it is imperative that contact is made with the Commission. Officials in the Commission exert a great deal of influence because the Commission is the only institution that can initiate and draft new legislation within the confines of the political priorities set by the Council of Ministers. Once drafted, however, the legislation has to be agreed by the parliament and the Council of Ministers and this is often a lengthy process of negotiation with compromises being reached. It is nevertheless important to bear in mind that the Commission is present at every stage of the institutional decision-making process, and plays an important role as a perceived 'honest broker'.

A drafts team will work on the proposals in the Commission before they are opened up to external consultations and often impact studies, full research into what the legislation will do, which then feed into the drafts. Each DG has its own position and these need to be taken into account when drafting, so a period of 'inter-service' consultation allows for the DG to look at, and influence, the proposals.

Lobbying on the proposals can come from a number of different perspectives but trade bodies carry much weight. These bodies are said to represent the voice of that industry and, therefore, they are listened to. This should not, and does not, prevent individual companies from lobbying and they are often able to make more pervasive points as they do not have to offer the balance, or compromise, of a trade body. Organizations will also often come together to argue in favour of a position. The European Union is often criticized for the power and influence wielded by consumer organizations and, in the same way that companies try to speak through a trade body, consumer groups are often able to champion the cause of the consumers across Europe.

When the legislation is presented to the parliament, it is what takes place behind the scenes that is often more important than the debates in the parliament. The political groups mentioned above can influence the priorities of the parliament. It is, however, the parliament's committees that do much of the detailed work on the legislation. Each committee has *rapporteurs* alongside the political membership, and they develop the legislation, often talk to outside groups and write a report.

It is often helpful to establish contact with your member state's permanent representation as they can act as a source of advice on lobbying tactics and assist in your understanding of the policymaking process and the stage that the policy that you are interested in has reached.

Whilst informal channels of communication exist between the European institutions, they are under no obligation to talk to each other as legislation progresses. Much of the contact that does take place depends on the personalities and any pre-existing relationships. This makes the role of lobbying much more important. External parties can assist in the development of legislation and it is very much the case that the participation of commercial bodies is welcome so they get it right.

It has to be remembered that not all policy initiatives in the European Union come to fruition. A policy may start to be developed but if it proves contentious, shown by the reaction generated, it can be dropped by the Commission. For this to happen a lot of lobbying needs to take place and a very good monitoring system needs to be in place as sometimes policy ideas do reappear several years later.

Once the legislation has been passed by the European institutions it is then up to each of the member states to implement it. This very often means lobbying each of the member states in how they implement the legislation to ensure that no 'gold-plating' takes place, ie that the member state does not go further in interpreting the scope of the legislation than was intended by the European institutions. Monitoring is a key element in any lobbying programme but this is especially the case in the European Union with so much policymaking taking place at any one time. It has been estimated that around 75 per cent of all legislation now originates from Europe. Waiting for the legislation to come from Europe and then start trying to influence it is simply too late, however important the implementation process actually is. Organizations need to be in Brussels, lobbying from the start of the process.

With the recent enlargement of the European Union to 25 countries, a new Constitution was put forward, one that could have altered Europe's institutions. The EU Constitution was agreed by EU member states at the European Council of 18 June 2004. It is a constitutional treaty containing important revisions and developments of the EU's institutions, competences, operating procedures and its relationship with the member states. It aims to incorporate transparency, greater democracy and efficiency into decision-making. The treaty was signed by all 25 EU member states in Rome on 29 October 2004. However, at the current time, the wording of the Constitution has been rejected by the electorates of France and the Netherlands meaning that the process is effectively 'on hold'.

But if we look at the wording of the Constitution it shows how Europe may develop over the coming years. If the member states were to ratify the text (or a version of it), the European Council would elect a *President* by qualified majority voting for a two-and-a-half-year term, renewable once. This president would lead and coordinate the work of the European Council and have a role as an external representative of the Union but with no executive powers. The presidency of the Council would be held on a rotating basis for periods of 18 months in order to maintain continuity of affairs. The Foreign Affairs Council would be the exception to this rule as it would be chaired by the new *EU Minister for Foreign Affairs*, who would be appointed by a qualified majority of member states. The Foreign Minister would combine the duties currently held by the EU External Relations Commissioner and the EU High Representative for the Common Foreign and Security Policy. This minister would also be one of the vice-presidents of the Commission.

Under the proposed Constitution, the qualified majority voting would become a standard voting method after 2009. The new rules stipulate that a decision would have to be backed by 55 per cent of the member states and that these would have to represent 65 per cent of the EU's total population. A minimum of four states would be needed to block a decision. Until 2014, the leadership of the European Commission would remain on the principle of one commissioner per member state. After 2014 this would be replaced by a system in which the number of commissioners corresponded to two-thirds of the number of member states, and the selection of commissioners would be based on a system of equal rotation among the member states. Following the ratification, the European Parliament's co-decision powers would be extended to judicial matters, policy cooperation and the agricultural policy. After 2009, the parliament would have a maximum of 750 members, regardless of the number of member states and no state would be given more than 96 or less than six seats.

If such changes were to be made in the structure of the EU these would have to be reflected when developing a lobbying programme.

It is the case though that when lobbying the EU you have to consider:

- the policymaking process;
- the position being taken by the political groups;
- the position being adopted by individual member states;
- the possibility of bringing member states together on an issue;
- getting involved as early as possible.

Brad Staples, Chairman, APCO Europe

The face of the EU has changed markedly in the past ten years – successive enlargements, more legislative powers at the EU level and a more open and transparent decision-making process. Successful lobbying in the EU is increasingly about understanding and knowing how to capitalize on these changes. Multi-country lobbying strategies campaigns are often essential to effecting real legislative change. These need to build on Brussels and member state insight, understanding and sensitivity to local politics, interests and behaviour. Success also depends on building sustained relationships and dialogue with Brussels officials and politicians over the five-year institutional cycle and the ability to come armed with solutions for policymakers rather than a catalogue of problems.

GLOBAL INSTITUTIONS

An increasing emphasis is being placed on the role of global institutions. Lobbying these institutions remains a somewhat under-explored avenue except for the very largest, usually multinational, companies. As problems, such as trade, environmental protection or the 'norms' of business behaviour require increasingly global attention, the role of these bodies can only increase. The World Bank and the World Trade Organization (WTO) will often interact directly with organizations and will work with the private sector on the implementation of their programmes.[13] Good relationships with these bodies take time to build and the way that your profile is enhanced will depend on their programmes and the role you want to play. In a similar way to working with individual states it is important to work with officials and those who head up your sector. If you are putting a policy argument to them the same rules apply about its accuracy and resonance, understanding the policymaking process and ensuring that it is well supported.

As an example, if we take the United Nations (UN) as another example of a global institution then if the General Assembly passes a resolution then an *ad hoc* committee can be established to look in more detail at the issue. The committee will be charged with producing a Treaty (relations between states) or a Convention (conduct within a state). It can take anywhere from several months to several years for a treaty to be established. From the perspective of a member of the UN, a resolution is, in effect, a guide to best practice and can be ignored or used accordingly; whereas a treaty should normally be complied with and many countries, such as the UK, usually do.

The pressure point for lobbyists, as this is similar for most global institutions, are the nation state members, to influence the position they adopt. Votes in the General Assembly require a two-thirds majority so demand a large degree of agreement. In an *ad hoc* committee, its members, drawn from the UN membership, will all take different positions reflecting the 'national line'.

Global institutions are bound to increase in number. Activists often campaign against these bodies because of their perceived lack of democratic accountability and this raises their profile. The policies of these bodies are often criticized and since the term globalization has become popular, the World Bank and WTO, in particular, have been said to be to blame for encouraging homogenized societies, overly powerful corporations and the exploitation of under-developed countries that globalization creates.

This should not denigrate the importance of domestic lobbying. Domestic lobbying is needed because:

- much international lobbying takes place through the national spokespeople or position of domestic politicians;
- many international bodies will consider the overall reputation of a company when dealing with it and this means getting the domestic politics right (see Chapter 6 on CSR);
- many international bodies will be more favourable to an organization that lobbies at all levels – they need to see that they are not the only ones being lobbied;
- international bodies often set some guidelines but the rest is up to national governments to implement so they need to have been aware of potential problems well in advance.

Mark Hatcher, Director, Cubitt Consulting (formerly Head of Global Public Affairs, PricewaterhouseCoopers)

Public affairs practitioners who advocate public policy solutions to meet the needs of a more integrated and interdependent, globalizing world need to pay much closer attention to multilateral bodies like the WTO, OECD or UNCTAD. This need will increase as political networks grow, public institutions and private interests interact more closely, and national governments and regulators collaborate to tackle cross-border, 'framework' issues.

Three simple top tips:
Keep informed: about the multilateral institutions.

Input your views: multilateral bodies increasingly provide opportunities for business and NGO involvement, in the interests of greater openness and transparency.
Call on national representations: locally-based officials can provide you with valuable 'on the ground' intelligence, as well as introductions to officials based in other representations.

GENERAL RULES:

- get involved as early as possible;
- build up contacts in advance of really needing them;
- have a monitoring system in place so you know what is going on;
- know the way that policy and decisions are made;
- ensure that you know who are the key people;
- build your argument and support it;
- pre-empt how you may be argued against and build in the defence mechanisms;
- be clear in what you are asking for;
- tailor your messages and your approach depending on who you are meeting;
- provide solutions where possible;
- know when to widen the scope of your lobbying, for instance by getting the opposition involved;
- always talk to the civil servants, do not go straight to the top without having first tried to raise your problem with those really doing the work.

Joe Brice, Government and Industry Affairs Manager, Schering

Know the environment:
An up to date understanding of the political environment you are operating in is imperative. This knowledge will enable you to tap into potential public affairs opportunities.

Know your objective:
What change are you hoping to bring about in your public affairs strategy? Remember to be realistic and create an accurate timescale.

Know your audience:
Public affairs is no longer focussed primarily on the Westminster Executive and legislature. Devolution has changed that. Public affairs is also more

than just government relations; patient organizations, advocacy groups, regulatory bodies and trade bodies should increasingly be taken into account.

Know what you want to say:
Think about the messages you want the particular audiences to take away, and tailor your materials accordingly.

Know your tactics:
The 'when and how' will vary immensely. Whatever tactics are agreed on, well-planned strategies are always flexible and able to react to the speed at which things change in politics.

WWF AND TRAFFIC'S WILDLIFE TRADE CAMPAIGN

Once illegal items enter the UK, inconsistencies in the law led to an anomaly whereby you could be arrested for poaching native endangered wildlife but you could not be arrested for selling the skin of a poached tiger, a rhino horn or a piece of ivory. This was because offences under the Control of Trade in Endangered Species (COTES) legislation were not arrestable. Lack of police powers ensured that risk of detection was low, and the often paltry fines made what risk there was even more lucrative. Together, these failures in law acted as no deterrent to wildlife trade criminals. WWF and its partner TRAFFIC (WWF's wildlife trade monitoring programme) campaigned to:

- secure primary legislation by the end of 2003 increasing the maximum penalty from two to five years, making illegal wildlife trade an arrestable offence;
- introduce sentencing guidelines for magistrates and judges that ensure the punishment fits the severity of the crime.

WWF and TRAFFIC embarked on a high-profile advocacy campaign to help raise awareness of the seriousness of the issue amongst political decision-makers. As the objective required primary legislation the initial focus was on Westminster and Whitehall either to secure space in the Criminal Justice Bill or a backbench (private member's) bill, which would introduce the changes to the law that they required.

Their strategy was to secure broad based, cross-party support and support from the relevant departments using hard line political messaging and topical debate to maintain interest and concern for this issue, to the extent that action was perceived to be necessary as a matter of urgency. The campaign:

- secured cross party support in parliament, which led to debates;
- recruited the support of individual political champions across the political spectrum who tabled debates, questions and bills to help maintain the pressure and momentum behind the campaign;
- secured a ten minute rule bill, a presentation bill and a private member's bill to promote the campaign;
- lobbied all major departments involved in the bill – DEFRA, the Home Office, the Lord Chancellor's Department and Number 10;
- researched and published five reports that had resonance with the target political audience, emphasising the impact of the trade on wildlife, and the links between wildlife crime and serious organized crime and repeat offenders;
- secured the support of influential stakeholders such as the Metropolitan Police Wildlife Crime Unit, and HM Customs and Excise;
- utilized the organization's supporters, activists and individual contacts to help secure parliamentary support and pressure on government departments;
- campaigned throughout the passage of the Criminal Justice Bill for amendments.

Throughout the period of intensive lobbying, letter writing and briefing, the media team maintained public interest and profile of the campaign through proactive and reactive media work. This resulted in national press coverage, for example, in the *Financial Times*, the *Independent* and the *Sun*, along with BBC and Sky breakfast news programmes, Radio Five Live and GMTV. This was bolstered by wide regional coverage that included ITV's *London Tonight* and *Scotland on Sunday*. In addition, TV chat shows picked up the story including the *Richard & Judy Show*.

The government was persuaded to table amendments to the Criminal Justice Bill at Committee stage in the Lords meaning that the final act contains measures making wildlife crime an arrestable offence and increases sentences from two to five years. Sentencing guidelines for magistrates have been introduced. In addition, the Metropolitan Police have also recruited two new wildlife officers to tackle the growing problem of wildlife crime in London.

The campaign adopted a broad approach to campaigning, utilizing all areas of communication to bolster the public affairs objective, including the media, supporters, online campaigners and celebrities.

BRITISH ASSOCIATION FOR ADOPTION AND FOSTERING (BAAF)

Connect Public Affairs was appointed by BAAF to assist them in successfully campaigning to amend the Adoption and Children Bill to allow unmarried couples to adopt. Government proposals to modernize adoption law did not intend to change previous (1976) legislation restricting the adoption rights to married couples and single persons only. BAAF needed to neutralize government opposition and demonstrate that it was necessary to increase the pool of those eligible to adopt.

The campaign decided to focus the debate on the issue of children's rights and welfare and distance it from gay rights and the relevance of the institution of marriage. Briefings highlighted the fact that unmarried couples already had the right to adopt but that the child was denied an equal legal relationship with both parents and that 5,000 new adoptive parents were needed each year.

A non-oppositional approach was adopted so that rather than call on the government to reverse their policy, BAAF campaigned for a free vote on an issue usually reserved to issues of morality. The campaign focused on winning strategic support for the campaign from all parties. Activity in the campaign included:

- a structured programme of contact and one-to-one meetings with civil servants, ministers and members of the special select committee and then standing committee;
- a cross party EDM tabled by Meg Munn MP, a former Deputy Director of Social Services, signed by over 130 MPs of all parties;
- securing the support of Conservative MPs for amendments tabled by a Labour MP.

Yet despite this the government was clearly not giving way and was resistant to calls for a free vote. The campaign moved into a period of short and intensive media focus to counter government concerns and proving that denying eligibility to unmarried (predominantly heterosexual) couples was equally unpopular.

BAAF briefed and targeted a small number of 'sympathetic' lobby and specialist correspondents and won articles and editorials over one weekend in the *Mirror*, *Guardian* and *Observer*. A feature article was also placed in *Tribune*. The *Evening Standard* then led on the story: 'Unmarried couples lose out as Blair dodges gay adoption row' and the front page of the *Daily Express* followed with 'BANNED: unmarried couples told they can't adopt.'

The *Evening Standard* and *Express* coverage provoked a reaction from the Downing Street Daily Press Briefing of 'Bollocks!' Subsequently, the government recognized the importance of permitting MPs to make individual decisions and agreed to a free vote. The prime minister and the whole Health front bench voted in favour and the measure was passed with a majority of 155.

Regardless of this success the bill, as amended, now lay vulnerable to opposition and a free vote in the Lords. A copy of 'Be My Parent', listing over 400 children who desperately needed to find adopted parents, was sent to all peers emphasising the importance of increasing the pool of adopters. With the issue of gay adoption preoccupying many peers, BAAF commissioned an opinion poll to establish that public opinion to gay adoption was favourable. This did not stop the Lords voting against it.

Iain Duncan Smith, then leader of the Conservative Party, imposed a three-line whip on Conservative members to oppose the amendment leading to his front bench colleague John Bercow resigning amongst media furore.

Another push was required when the bill went back to the Lords and BAAF utilized its wide membership to present its case in conjunction with children's charities at an eleventh hour briefing meeting. Baroness Gould, their champion peer, personally encouraged Labour peers to turn up and vote. Whilst the numbers against remained the same, those in favour increased. The campaign was won by 215 votes to 184.

The government was initially opposed to the amendment but as a result of successful lobbying BAAF were able to secure and win a free vote in the Commons, ensure it went back to the Lords after it was defeated and achieve a historic victory in the Upper House. This programme demonstrates the clear need to understand all stages of the parliamentary progress of a bill.

Endnotes

1. Indeed, the opposite can also be said – a number of current MPs were previously employed as lobbyists.
2. For a more detailed discussion on stakeholders please refer to Chapter 5.
3. Early Day Motions are expressions of parliamentary support for an issue. An MP, or number of MPs, can put down an EDM and then collect signatories to it. The higher the number of signatories the more influence it may have. The wording of the EDM is up to the MP putting it down.
4. The membership of select committees is made up of backbench MPs. Each committee mirrors the major departments of government and

undertakes inquiries as a parliamentary check on the Executive. Select committees call for written evidence and also take oral evidence sessions. They have the power to force people to appear before the committee to give evidence. Once the inquiry is complete, the committee will issue a report and the government has to respond formally to this report.

5. All Party Groups of parliamentarians are based on either issue or country lines, eg the All Party Beer Group or the All Party Africa Group. Parliamentarians join the group to enable it to gain a higher profile and the groups often hold meetings where they can hear from experts in the field and discuss the topic in more detail. Each group has a number of office holders – secretary, chair etc.
6. For a much more detailed examination of the parliamentary process see Childs, S (2002) *Politico's Guide to Parliament*, Politico's Publishing, London
7. See Chapter 4 for a fuller discussion of issues-led campaigns.
8. See Chapter 3 for a fuller discussion of the use of media relations.
9. Chapter 3 contains more detail on the role of media monitoring.
10. For more information on the media see Chapter 3, and for information on party conference see Chapter 4.
11. See Chapter 5 on stakeholder relations.
12. Although recent changes have increased the Assembly's powers.
13. For many critics of the World Bank and the WTO, their relationships with the private sector are too close and they are often criticized for placing the need for profit above the needs of the citizens they should be protecting and helping.

3

Reputation and the media

The media's importance in public affairs is constantly increasing. Those who have been involved in the industry for many years have seen this change and whereas they may not have dealt with the media in early campaigns, they certainly have to now. The growth in importance of the media may seem a very straightforward and uncontroversial statement but there are a number of ways in which it can impact on a campaign. It is, therefore, important that those advising on public affairs also understand the demands and ways of the working of the media. Working with the media is different from working with politicians.

In the first instance we have to be clear in knowing what we mean by the media. This will vary depending on the nature of the public affairs programme but can include:

- the national broadsheet press;
- the tabloid press;
- regional newspapers;
- local newspapers including the free sheets;
- national TV including satellite broadcasters;
- national radio;
- local TV;

- local radio;
- specialist and trade publications.

You may not be working with all these various media outlets on a particular campaign but each can have an impact. The media can be important in the following ways, and all these need to be considered as part of your public affairs activity:

- making the issue more 'public' with an increased profile;
- carrying adverse comments about your organization;
- dealing with the aftermath of a crisis.

Often media relations are about protecting the good name and reputation of your organization and individuals, probably senior, within the organization. When campaigning for change, maybe through legislation, then you need to ensure that:

- your organization has a good name;
- senior executives have a good name;
- crises are dealt with quickly and with the minimum of damage to reputation;
- politicians have a good impression of your organization.

MEDIA RELATIONS

Some sectors more than others are greatly affected by the actions of politicians and the government. These are often those sectors that are heavily regulated, such as healthcare, telecommunications, financial services etc. Those sectors with an increasingly high media profile, such as food, find themselves under the spotlight of political scrutiny, as the 'something must be done' attitude takes hold.

How the three corners of the triangle formed by the public, the media and the political community interact with, reflect, refract, condition and feed off and into one another is beyond this chapter, and has been the subject of some fairly heavyweight academic analysis. They should not even be considered as separate and discrete from each other, but it makes it easier to consider them so. Indeed, discussions about the nature of these relationships are essentially discussions about what actually constitutes politics, with a small 'p', in today's world. There has always been a clear level of interplay between the three but the rise of the 24-hour media has made it even clearer in the modern environment.[1]

The rise of the 24-hour media has brought with it increased competition between news outlets for exclusive stories. The media fight over new and differing angles on stories in an attempt to gain viewers or readers. This has alerted the media to the behaviour of organizations, especially in the corporate sector, as bad or unethical behaviour makes a good story. The rise of the brand, and the role that brands play in people's lives day to day, has also placed organizations in the glare of the media, making them 'fair game'. The actions of executives at Enron, WorldCom and others has shown the media that corporate behaviour needs covering and many senior personnel openly court media attention and thrive in the media spotlight. There is also the rise of the activist. These activists are, they would claim, trying to force organizations to behave in an ethical manner. Activists target organizations in a number of ways, and are very effective in their media relations.[2]

Suffice to say the public, politicians and the media are intrinsically linked and none can be dealt with in isolation. A member of parliament or a local councillor, or even a regulator, is influenced by the press's treatment of an issue. Public opinion is also conditioned, some even say determined, by the media. You also have to factor in the variety of media now available and how they may have their own agendas on a particular issue.

The media can be influenced by what a politician says, as can the public. And politicians do, of course, mostly try to be reflective of their *perception* of their constituents' opinions, which, again are often presented to them in a mediated form, rather than through direct contact. Although technology is increasingly empowering more 'direct' contact, it can often be manipulated to put forward unrepresentative opinions as representative.

In essence, what media relations activity often tries to achieve as part of a public affairs programme is:

- pressure on politicians – working with the media to make your issue a news story, to try to apply pressure on politicians (usually the government) so that they are forced to do something about it;
- the support of the public which, obviously, assists in the achievement of the first – making your issue one that chimes with the public and making them aware of the matter through the media.

The activity has to fit with your overall strategy and you need to be aware of what the coverage may lead to, or what the pitfalls may be. There is no point getting a story in the newspapers for the sake of it; this would achieve little and may merely serve to alienate potential supporters.

You are setting out to secure media coverage and then try to allow the story to run and grow and develop without, necessarily, you having too much more involvement.

In a similar way to when you are writing a briefing paper for a politician, your first actions should be to make sure that the story you are trying to sell to the media 'stacks up'. This should mean that it:

- is one that the journalist will be attracted to;
- will appeal to the audience of the media you are approaching;
- will not leave the journalist exposed to criticism for being inaccurate;
- will have the effect you desire on government.

Your first task should be to identify the media that ideally you would like to work with on your story. To do this you need to understand the type of story you are working with – it may be a political story, it may be more appropriate for a business audience, or perhaps you are dealing with a matter that only a more specialized audience will comprehend.

When you have been through this process this will help you to identify both the publication and the journalist you should target.

There are specialist databases available that can help you in this process – Mediadisk is well regarded and offers the contact details of thousands of journalists across the range of media, local, national and specialist press. Also available to members is the CIPR *Media Directory*, which is accessible in the member area/information centre of www.cipr.co.uk. Other directories include *BRAD*.

The next step is to decide what it is you are trying to 'sell in' to the journalist. You have to fully understand your story and why it is the journalist should be attracted to it. When you telephone the journalist that you have identified, you will only have a very short amount of time to tweak his or her interest and sell them your story.[3] Journalists are very busy and invariably under pressure, so make the best of the short time that you will have with them. Do a press search on their previous articles to know what they have written about recently, the type of angles they take, as this will help you. It may also reveal if the journalist should be approached at all, maybe he or she has taken an opposite view in the past to the one you are trying to sell at the current time. You have also to understand the priorities of the government and the type of story that will resonate with them – are there particular priorities to be met, or worries that the government has with which you need to frame your approach.

To increase your chances of success, write yourself a script that explains:

- The nature of the story – who, what, when, where?
- Why this is a story – why should anyone be interested in it, the 'so what' factor?
- What is the impact of the story?

You have to be giving the journalist a story that no one else has or, at least, some new information on a story. Journalists are professionals and should be treated as such; never approach them without having done your homework. You will only get one shot at talking to them and you have to make the most of that opportunity.

To do this you also need to know when to call them or, more importantly, when not to call them. This means knowing the publication and its deadlines – do not call the journalists when a deadline is looming, they will not have time to talk to you and if you call them at this time you may create a bad impression. Obviously when dealing with the broadcast media their deadlines are more constant but they remain under pressure.

Everyone's style of 'sell-in' varies and you will develop your own style with experience, but you could conduct the call in the following way:

- Hello, is that Joe Journo?
- My name is Rob and I am calling from Acme Ball Bearings. I've got a story that I thought you might be interested in. Have you got time to talk to me about it at the moment?
- That's great. I've got a story about the government's plans to abolish income relief on new ball bearings. Well obviously UK manufacturing is going through a difficult time at the moment, but this move will kill the industry in the UK and will lead to hundreds of job losses.
- I wondered if this is the sort of story that might interest you?

Journalists will want to ask you for more information if their interest is tweaked so you have to have thought like a journalist when preparing for the call and when writing your script – what type of question will they ask and what sort of information will they need? Once you have convinced journalists that you have a story, then you have only got over the first hurdle. Be ready for them to ask you to send the details to them and always expect for them to do their own research on the story; never expect them simply to take your word for it. In fact, if possible, always allow enough room in your story for journalists to make their own mark, take your story and develop it still further. This sense of ownership can only help. If you are dealing with the broadcast media then you will also need to think about visuals for the story, and with the radio an interview that would accompany the story. Images are incredibly useful for the print media and, if you can, offer them some images that may help you secure the coverage. However, such images do need to be of a good quality. The way in which you supply information to journalists will depend on the story – you may e-mail them a formal statement that they can quote, you may send a number of bullet points summarizing your argument or you may need to send a press release.

Be sure to check how they like their materials to be delivered – e-mail or fax? If you are sending an e-mail then you may need to send it as plain text, not an attachment as these can sometimes be blocked by e-mail security systems. If you do 'cut and paste' a press release into an e-mail then do not include logos as this, again, may cause the e-mail to be blocked by security systems.

Writing a press release requires skill in neatly summarizing the story you are trying to sell and there are several 'dos and don'ts' when writing them.

Do:

- keep the press release, ideally, to one side A4 in length;
- chose a snappy title that catches the attention of the reader;
- summarize your main point in the first paragraph of the release – keep this paragraph short;
- include a quote;
- include contact details for more information;
- include notes to editors that provide some background information.

Do not:

- extend the explanation of your story;
- go into too much detail;
- expect a high level of understanding from the reader;
- always send the same press release to everyone – you may need to tailor it depending on the audience;
- use too many technical or over-complicated terms.

Again with press releases, as with other approaches to journalists, you need to know who you are sending it to and understand the nature and audience of the publication.

All being well, when all of this has taken place, you will have achieved the coverage desired. If you secured the story on behalf of a client or the senior management then be sure to have a copy of the coverage, ideally on the day of its publication, or a tape of the broadcast. When sending this around, be sure to note:

- the name of the outlet;
- its circulation or viewing figures;
- how this fits into your public affairs campaign and what your next steps are.

If the story needs to continue then be on the look out for new angles and developments that you could give to the media. You may wish to work with the same journalist or to try to build a network of contacts by giving the new outlet the information. Stories can run and run, while others feature heavily and then simply fade away. Once again, by ensuring that you are clear in your strategy before commencing this process you will know how you would like your story to play out. You also need to have considered, right from the outset, what you are looking to achieve from the coverage and how this impacts on the other parts of the public affairs activity.

Obviously, the above concentrates on selling a story to the media but media relations in public affairs can also use a number of different approaches to supporting your campaign. Media relations can also include:

- Letter writing – this is very useful when considering local media outlets and trying to raise the profile of your issue. Letters can come from your organization or, if trying to show widespread support for your position, others should be encouraged to write in. If the matter you are dealing with is very local then residents, community members etc should be taking part in letter writing.
- Responding to news stories – if articles in the press are hostile to your position or convey inaccurate information then it can be important to respond to them. This could be in the form of a letter to the editor of the newspaper, in a press release that 'puts the record straight' or in a reply article working with the same journalist who wrote the original article.
- Penned articles – opinion pieces from a senior representative in your organization can assist in highlighting your issue and can also raise the profile of that individual. This can be of use when you are working with political audiences to show that you have the expertise that can assist in policymaking.

Once the coverage has been generated, the most important element is how you capitalize on it and ensure that it helps to deliver your public affairs programme.

You should continue to engage with government so that you are seen to be providing the answers to a problem that has arisen, and its associated media coverage etc. The story may need to be anonymous, ie unrelated to your organization, otherwise government may take action against your position. This would need to be considered before coverage is sought.

Be flexible enough in making your arguments to government to learn from the coverage, for instance from comments that are made by others or the main criticisms of government. Do not keep your arguments static. If the story grows and develops, let your strategy and arguments develop. They should not remain in aspic.

Think creatively about the ways that you can use the coverage, do not just think about the direct application of pressure on government think also about:

- generating support from others – either in supportive quotes or getting them to lobby government on the matter;

- following up on leads generated by the coverage – there may be avenues that you have not considered to date as part of the strategy, eg potential supporters;
- following up with supporters or potential supporters – writing letters to them on the back of the coverage.

Whilst the above details are concerned primarily with a news story that may appeal to the media, there are many types of news story and you should not concentrate solely on those that criticize existing policy or the government. The types of coverage that could benefit your public affairs strategy could include:

- a new report released;
- statistics about your sector;
- a general announcement about the company, eg profits or sales figures;
- comments from a senior business leader or someone in your own organization;
- using a government announcement to base follow up comments or an article, such as the Queen's Speech, the Budget, a new policy announcement or government statistics;
- using a political or future event to build your strategy on, eg an anniversary or celebration.

The role of the media is increasingly a component of a fully developed public affairs strategy and needs to be fundamental to its development.

CRISIS MANAGEMENT

There are many reasons why a crisis should be dealt with quickly and any impact minimized. They can have a number of implications across an organization but from the perspective of public affairs there are a number of very clear reasons why crises need to be planned for and dealt with to protect your organization.[4] In particular:

- politicians can react to crisis by making adverse comments;
- politicians can react to a crisis by making policy on the hoof;
- a crisis can undermine the name and reputation of the company and thereby damage relations with government;
- adverse comment can damage relations with politicians more generally;
- a crisis can bring regulatory pressures in heavily regulated industries;

- you need to develop 'friends' in advance of a crisis and these friends will include politicians and government.

The management of media relations and communications is becoming a top priority in public affairs. In a crisis situation an organization has to protect its reputation so doing nothing is not an option. The same is true when an organization faces a less explosive but more long-term problem. A reputation takes time, effort and a lot of money to develop. A damaged reputation can swiftly destroy consumer and investor confidence, employee morale, competitive advantage and the trust of political audiences. Once lost, a reputation may never be rebuilt. At best, it can take many years.

If the media is not dealt with effectively then you risk:

- brand damage;
- poor employee morale;
- loss of consumer confidence;
- falling share price and poor investor relations;
- problems with supplier relations;
- career and personal implications;
- a regulatory or legislative reaction to public pressure.

Obviously the consequences will vary depending on the nature of the organization and of the type of crisis, but it is clear that they are significant.

Dealing with a crisis means closely coordinating all elements of communications, and increasingly noting the legal environment. There can be legal constraints on communications activity, depending on the stage of proceedings, eg if the crisis is caused by a dawn raid by a regulatory authority, if a criminal prosecution is possible, or if there are redundancies involved that could lead to future legal liabilities.

The first stage in a crisis has to be to verify the nature of the situation – what has happened and where – and to start the process of gathering information about the situation. Prepare an initial statement and key messages and tailor them in terms of content and delivery to your key audiences – these should be identified in advance. There is no need to feel you must have all the answers straight away, but it is vital that you open up lines of communication with all of your stakeholders as a matter of urgency and think about what they will want to know. It is essential to commit publicly to communicating openly and frankly with them.

In terms of the media, often it is best to prepare a holding statement that should contain:

- a brief outline of what is happening;
- who you have informed;

- what immediate action you are taking;
- when you may know more.

The major consideration is whether you may need to apologize for the incident or to those involved.

You will need to implement mechanisms to monitor events as they unfold; this can be in part achieved by opening up lines of communication with the key stakeholders. You will need to put media monitoring procedures in place to ensure that you are aware of what, if anything, is being reported in print and broadcast media. It is important that you are able and prepared to react to events as they unfold. You should also begin preparing your key briefing materials to cope with queries as the process continues, including 'question and answer' documents and more detailed press statements.

The issue of stakeholders is dealt with in Chapter 5, but in a crisis situation, these stakeholders should be engaged and it is preferable that lines of communication are established with all audiences as soon as possible to minimize distortion and misinterpretation of events. Consideration should be given to the best method of communication with each group, and the best people to manage that communication. In an ideal world, you will already have established good relations with these audiences well in advance and this can prevent negative comment in the event of a crisis. A proactive communications programme to introduce your organization in advance to key political figures including local ones should be established – in short you would have established a line of goodwill. However this is not always the case but that does not mean that contact, in the event of a crisis, should not take place.

It is vitally important to manage as much as possible who is communicating what with the media and ensuring everyone is 'singing from the same hymn sheet' to avoid potential confusion or misrepresentation. With this is in mind, you need to be aware that anything that is said to an audience may be given or leaked to the media. It is imperative that when communicating with any audience that this is borne in mind.

Elected representatives should be communicated with at the earliest possible opportunity. They are normally significant opinion formers and opinion leaders locally, and sometimes nationally as well. They will often be asked to comment in the media about a high-profile incident and it is essential that they have heard your version of events directly. Furthermore, they may contact you directly, at any time, to find out what is going on but may comment publicly before they do that.

In relation to an incident that took place in Scotland, coverage was generated nationally about comments from the local MP, for instance 'Time bomb; Factory Disasters: Warnings Ignored' published in the *Sun*, 13 May 2004:

> Maryhill MP Ann McKechin told last night how she had been compiling a dossier of complaints from workers at the plant since last year. The MP – who visited the site with Jack McConnell yesterday – said: 'I'd been dealing with complaints about the health and safety environment in the factory. The main complaint was about the lack of suitable protective clothing. It certainly seems there wasn't a formal mechanism that allowed the reporting of safety concerns.'

The key political figures will depend on the scale of the crisis but as a general rule, your local MP should always be kept informed (and the MPs of anyone else involved, if these are different), as should local ward councillors. You should always be aware that what can start as a local issue can often become a national political issue. This is particularly a risk close to local or general elections, within a closely divided council or when there are political differences between local and national representatives. If you explain the circumstances fully, your councillors and member of parliament can often play valuable intermediary roles.

In particularly high profile incidents, one would also want to open communication with national representatives additional to the local MP, most prominently the minister with responsibility for your industry.

Other key groups to communicate with will include employees, trade unions, trade associations or representative bodies and also peers and their organizations. You may need some friends, independent voices to speak up for you as the incident unfolds. Such contacts should be identified, preferably in advance, and kept informed about developments.

In relation to the media, it is crucial to identify the key publications for the area concerned, the journalists who would normally deal with your issues and their direct contact numbers. You should always assume that there will be media attention, at least locally, and quite possibly nationally if the incident is significant. The specialist media is rarely as time sensitive as local and national media, if only because of the frequency of the publication.

Those speaking on behalf of your organization should be media-trained and prepared to speak directly to the media; however there are significant risks with undertaking 'live' media interviews. Well-managed, they can make a positive contribution to the management of a crisis; however, they bring with them significant risks. The decision to undertake 'live' interviews should only be taken in the context of the legal and communications strategy and it is often not the best use of time in the heat following a crisis. Communications immediately following a crisis are normally best managed through written statements, but one alternative would be for the spokesperson to deliver orally a written statement. Even if no interviews are being conducted, all senior staff should act naturally when going about their business, as they could be approached by the media at any time.

They should not act evasively or obviously seek to avoid journalists; they should be polite and say that unfortunately they are not able to comment at the present time. Investigations, either internal or external are useful holding tools in this regard.

Being in the media spotlight is unpleasant and worrying. Facing cameras or a microphone with questions being thrown at you can be testing and mistakes can cost the reputations you are trying to protect. Preparing for contact with the media is essential if a spokesperson is to put across his or her views effectively and with confidence, and is able to deal with the questions that will come. Media training is, therefore, an essential element in the preparation for a crisis and should cover print, TV and radio. It should provide participants with improved media handling skills, and increased confidence and competency when facing journalists.

Ideally, those at the top of your organization should be available to act as spokespersons in the event of a major crisis; from the perspective of the media and political audiences you have to be seen to be taking it seriously and dealing with it at the most senior level.

Media training will often include:

- practical interviews following a number of scenarios;
- a variety of interviewing styles;
- advice on preparing for interviews;
- work on how to communicate key messages;
- an explanation of the tactics used by interviewers.

For the team dealing with the press calls your attitude to media on the premises or on the telephone should always be courteous and helpful. A dedicated telephone number, normally staffed by a member of the communications team and available 24 hours a day should be given to journalists.

When media calls start to come in there are a number of 'dos and don'ts' for those authorized to deal with them on a particular issue.

You must:

- Have a pre-agreed press release, 'Q&A' and key messages to hand. These will form the script used when speaking to journalists to avoid mistakes or embarrassing omissions.
- Carefully log all calls – with name, publication, telephone number, fax number, e-mail, nature of query, deadline.
- Always be friendly and helpful when receiving calls – even if the journalist is asking difficult questions.
- Return calls, and if there is to be any delay in dealing with a request from journalists, let them know.

- When journalists ask for information try and get it if possible. This may not always be appropriate but it does help minimize the possibility of adverse comment.
- If a journalist asks for an interview, even though it is known internally that they will not get one, make sure it appears that an attempt is made.
- Give a name if a journalist asks for it, but insist on being called a 'spokesperson' if quoted.
- Promptly provide easily available material, for example the press release.
- Never promise more than can actually be delivered.
- Check if you need a press cutting service and broadcast monitoring. This will help to keep full track of the issue.
- Know your way around the company being dealt with – get the contact details of key people who may help as sources of information.
- If making announcements about a person/appointment/resignation etc then have information about that person available – age, previous occupations etc.
- Provide regular feedback (eg during a large announcement or ongoing crisis, at least four times a day) – you may need to provide reassurance, as others in the organization need to know what is being done, and you may well need to demonstrate the value of activity to senior levels.

Overall, the golden rules of dealing with the media when selling a story or dealing with a crisis are:

- If you ring a journalist make sure you call him or her at a time that suits their deadlines.
- Make sure you understand what the journalist will want from the story.
- If you are talking to a journalist NEVER LIE.
- When appearing on TV never let your eyes wander. People will not trust you.
- Work out what you want to say – and stick to it like glue.
- Do not believe the journalist is your friend, even if the journalist is friendly.
- Do not be more concerned about dealing with the tabloids than the broadsheets. Be concerned about BOTH.
- Never to talk to a journalist 'off the record'. There is no such thing and you may still be quoted.

Part of any good public affairs campaign should also assist organizations to prepare for a crisis. The better prepared you are the less likely it is to have a major adverse impact. As indicated at several stages above, lining up the information and details in advance can be a real advantage. Putting a crisis management plan in place can assist in the smooth running of the operation if something does go wrong. The plan should be short and concise but should be fully 'road tested' to make sure it works. The plan needs to include:

- who is responsible for leading the crisis team;
- who is included in the crisis team;
- contact numbers for those in the crisis team;
- who is responsible for talking to the media (this would involve media training in advance as well);
- details of any outside advisers involved – lawyers, communications consultants etc;
- details of stakeholders;
- details of appropriate media contacts.

In preparing the plan you should also have identified areas of potential crisis for the organization, to help address any potential weak spots but also to inform your plan. This could include the impact of future legislation, a failure to comply with current requirements, 'gaps' in current provision, failures of internal systems, past crises that have not been dealt with effectively, attacks by activist groups, a lack of a corporate social responsibility strategy etc. The range of possible crises is endless but it helps to obtain ideas from throughout the organization where the possible sources are so that you can put the necessary preparations, or maybe even remedies, in place.

FOR THE SAKE OF THE CHILDREN – TAKING RESPONSIBILITY FOR CHILD PROTECTION

When Lauren Wright, aged six, died at the hands of her parents after errors by social workers in Norfolk County Council and others failed to protect her, the council decided that the responsible action was to resist the call for someone to be blamed for the tragedy. Whilst accepting that its social workers had made mistakes, the council decided, even in the face of what it knew would come their way from many quarters, to make the case for the profession.

Given the background to the case, there was never any doubt that Norfolk Social Services would come in for severe and justifiable criticism and that there would be an intense media spotlight. In planning their approach, the communications team took account of a number of facts:

- at least one child a week dies at the hands of a relative;
- this was the fourth high-profile death of a child in Norfolk – all killed by their carers;
- other child abuse cases were making headlines;
- the team manager who had made a mistake in the case had resigned almost immediately.

The communications team's rationale was:

- This was not a case of system failure but of human error.
- There were professional issues that posed greater threats to the service and management of risks in child protection.
- Public perception and recognition of the value of social workers was very low.
- It was recognized by the council's members, clients and the government that they provided a good service to local people and had in place improvement plans for the weaker areas.
- A high-profile sacking or resignation may shorten the pain in the short term, but serve only to damage and destabilize the service in the long term.

The approach adopted was to:

- inform and educate;
- target responsible media, brief and pre-negotiate;
- apologize;
- explain;
- campaign.

When dealing with the media this meant:

- owning up to errors;
- no resignations;
- no identification of the team manager – explain, do not blame;
- no 'finger pointing' across the agencies;
- political and corporate commitment.

As this was a criminal case with a trial involved, there were three clear stages to the activity.

Pretrial:

- promoting and achieving good local media coverage;
- preparing background information;
- agreeing clear communication protocols with all partners;
- briefing key staff in social services;
- agreeing practical procedures to protect and support some very vulnerable staff;
- briefing members, MPs, government departments, relevant professional bodies and agencies.

During the trial:

- preparing and testing a Q & A's and rehearsing spokespersons;
- briefing target media nationally and locally selectively and negotiated print and broadcast features for the day and week of the verdict.

Post trial:

- arranging a press conference where their director made a statement in which he spelled out openly and honestly the mistakes that had been made and apologized for them;
- working with BBC Radio 4 on a week-long snapshot series following social workers and interviewing key staff;
- encouraging and facilitating follow-up features;
- publishing evidence to the Climbie Inquiry based on lessons learned in Norfolk and elsewhere.

Unsurprisingly the council's failures were reported widely and earned them the expected share of bad press. Unison (trade union), however, commended the council for the way they had supported staff while still taking responsibility for the errors made and the council's reputation as a good and supportive place to work was increased.

The coverage was in the main fair, balanced and accurate and included strong features on context, the scale and nature of problems for child protection and explored issues of agency and community responsibilities.

The way in which this crisis was handled shows the need to understand the demands of the media and the reassurance that the public requires, alongside the ability to defend a position and argue it. To do this needs knowledge about the background to the case and where the lines of media interest will come from and how to answer them.

Michael Regester, founding Director of Regester Larkin, and co-author, with Judy Larkin, of *Risk Issues and Crisis Management*, one of the CIPR's *In Practice* series

When a crisis occurs, people's initial sense of shock often turns to anger if the company at the centre of the crisis is not seen to take the appropriate action or to say the appropriate words. If it is able to communicate a message acknowledging the crisis, what they intend to do with it and how they feel about it, then the anger will be dispelled.

Whether written or spoken, statements must always cover the following topics in the following order: people, environment, property and money. This is the order in which most newspapers and broadcast media will cover the story. Remember; don't blame the media for your problems.

'DOMESTIC VIOLENCE: IT'S A MATTER OF LIFE AND DEATH'

Refuge, the not-for-profit organization that provides help and advice for women suffering from domestic abuse and violence, recognized there was a general lack of awareness of the services it offers and that more could be done to assist women who required specialized help. They also needed to increase funding in order to be able to expand their services. The intention of this campaign was also to provide victims of domestic violence with information about the services offered by Refuge and to change the attitudes of these sufferers from passivity to self-assurance. The campaign had to confront the victims' fear of speaking out, and to reinforce Refuge's position as a professional support group.

Violence in the home is an area the media has in the past stayed clear of. The challenge was, therefore, to educate the public about this social ill via the media, gather opinion against such acts of violence and to portray Refuge as an organization with a positive role in society.

Working with Oasis Media, Refuge realized that the campaign had to address the problem of domestic violence by getting issues talked about and ensure continuing public interest over a long period. Oasis Media proposed that the campaign's direction should focus on the immediate dangers of domestic violence and decided on the theme 'Domestic Violence: It's a matter of life and death', emphasizing the real physical threat sufferers in these situations face. Being an emotive issue, there was also the danger of 'sentimentalizing' domestic violence and it was crucial that the programme projected the appropriate ideas. The campaign targeted:

- media;
- press;
- broadcast (television and radio);
- opinion formers;
- government and the legislative community;
- social services;
- the police;
- the general public.

The media element of the campaign had a number of elements:

- Press – a wide range of newspapers was targeted for the campaign in order to reach as many readers as possible. A deal with the *Sun* was negotiated and it agreed to champion the cause on the proviso that they received an exclusive interview with Sheryl Gascoigne, footballer Paul Gascoigne's battered wife. A special 'You the Jury' telephone poll in the *Sun* was arranged to help draw readers into the campaign. Celebrity endorsement came from the likes of Ruby Wax, Lorraine Kelly, Helen Mirren, Julia Sawalha, Kathy Lette and Cherie Booth QC. Interviews with Sheryl were also secured with broadsheets like the *Observer* and the *Independent*.
- Broadcast – Sheryl Gascoigne was interviewed by Trevor McDonald on ITV's *Tonight*. News about Refuge's campaigning activities also made it into ITV's *This Morning*, the talk show *Trisha* and Gloria Hunniford's *Open House* on Channel 5.
- Advertising – working *pro bono* with ad agency Grey Advertising, a series of TV and print advertisements were designed and produced.
- Promotion – To meet the fundraising needs, a campaign hallmark was chosen – a black and white ribbon to symbolize life and death. A substantial donation from the *Sun* was obtained to help finance production of the ribbons, which were sold in every Waterstone's store in the UK.
- Internet – A campaign web page was secured on Waterstone's website.

Total coverage figures exceeded 140 million opportunities for people to see or hear about the campaign. Coverage spanned the majority of national dailies, national radio, regional and local media. The National Lottery Charities Board injected a grant of £247,000 into Refuge in support of the campaign. Contributions to Refuge via *Sun* readers amounted to over £40,000.

The Refuge 24-hour helpline was flooded with telephone calls, and both Refuge and the *Sun* were overwhelmed with over 3,000 calls for campaign ribbons, as well as offers of long-term practical and financial support.

Of the *Sun* readers who phoned in for the 'You the Jury' poll , 89 per cent thought Sheryl was right to expose her husband's violent behaviour. The campaign encouraged other victims of violent domestic abuse, such as Ulrika Jonsson and Glenda Jackson to come forward with their own experiences.

This campaign shows the importance of a partnership approach and how different strands of a media campaign can deliver results.

Michael Bland, Michael Bland Communication Consultancy, author of *When It Hits The Fan*

When a crisis strikes, instead of thinking what you want to tell your all-important audiences, put yourself in the minds of your audiences – the frightened local resident or consumer, the journalist with a deadline, the opportunist politician, the outraged customer, the mildly unhinged pressure group campaigner – and ask yourself: 'If I were that person, what would I want this company to do and say?'

OK, you may not be able to do and say all they want – perhaps you're not as guilty as they think, for example – but *their expectations* should be the starting benchmark for your crisis communications.

Endnotes

1. In Colin Clifford's (2002) *The Asquiths*, John Murray, London, there is a fantastic insight into Lloyd George's briefing of the press to put his position in the best light, and this is the early years of the twentieth century, around 100 years ago!
2. For a discussion on the behaviour and activity of activists and how companies have responded to the challenge, see John, S and Thomson, S (eds) (2003), *New Activism and the Corporate Response*, Palgrave, London.
3. The term 'sell in' and 'sell' your story, does not mean for money!
4. The CIPR has produced *Risk Issues and Crisis Management* (2005), Kogan Page, London, as a complete guidebook to dealing with crises. This section is shorter and concentrates more on the political impact of a crisis as well. We have, however, remained consistent with Regester/ Larkin's earlier edition, have employed some of their writing but have also put our work in a public affairs setting.

4

Managing issues

Issues management is not simply about the delivery of messages to political or media audiences. It is, instead, about understanding the issues, building and developing them and then presenting them in a way that will secure support for your cause or campaign.

This can present significant challenges as some issues may appear simply too difficult to 'sell' or too complicated to understand for anyone other than those completely specialist in the area. This is not the case. Public affairs consultants need to be able to work on a range of issues sometimes outside their immediate range of experience. At such times it is important that they rely on their public affairs expertise and work their way through the problem. Of course, those employed 'in-house' will be able to hone their skills and expertise and become specialists whereas many of those involved in consultancy may be more generalist.

The chapter on lobbying describes the writing of briefing papers and the content of those papers. This chapter deals more with the issues themselves and the options open to those involved in public affairs in securing a favourable outcome.

GET TO THE HEART OF THE ISSUE

It is not uncommon to be approached by a client, be they internal or external, with an issue that they know to be of concern but whose understanding ends there. It is the role of those involved in public affairs to help them explore the issue in more detail, decide what outcome they are seeking and then assist in framing the argument.

Under these circumstances a golden rule is to be realistic. It can be at this early stage that expectations are built to such an extent that the campaign is always doomed to failure because these are not met. It is not unusual to hear:

- 'We'll get the government to drop this bill.'
- 'I know the adviser in Number 10 and he will make sure the government drops this idea.'
- 'This policy is going to cost us so much money, we need the government to see sense.'

Be prepared to challenge those who come to you with a 'reality check' about what is, and is not, achievable. It does not matter whether you work 'in-house' or for a consultancy there is no easier way to disappoint and lose a client or a supporter than to over-promise.

However, before you can work out what is realistic to expect, you need to be able to understand the issue and have worked out your plan of action, complete with aims. To be able to do this fully you need to research the issue. This means really trying to get to grips with the matter and reading round it. Often the best way to do this is to talk to others. For those 'in-house', identify and talk to relevant people in the organization; for consultants, talk to immediate colleagues. Often, similar problems may have been encountered in the past and their expertise can help guide you. Never be too proud to talk to others and never believe that you alone have all the answers. Ideas can, and should, come from all levels in a team or organization and elements of an issue that you do not understand, others may.

Once you begin to understand the issue, you need to understand the problem – what is it that needs to be solved through lobbying and communications activity? The preferred option is always to offer a solution to the problem and if you can consider this towards the start of the process then you increase your chances of finding that solution.

To be able to offer a solution you have to gain an insight into how your intended audience, normally the government, will react. You can only know this by understanding the position being adopted by the government and by key individuals, and how your issue fits into the government's overall agenda. For instance, if a company wanted to argue for the abolition of the minimum wage, how would the current Labour Government react? – 'badly' would be an understatement, but how do you know this? The answer is to research the background to the issue with government:

- Has government issued any statements?
- What did these statements say?
- Has the prime minister or other senior minister spoken or made a speech on the issue?
- Has it been the subject of a parliamentary debate, as this would have included a ministerial statement on the matter?
- Did the party say anything about this issue in its last manifesto?
- Has the minister said anything in the press?

Be prepared to speak to those making the policy, eg the bill team for a parliamentary bill, to get an understanding of where they are coming from and the pressures they face. The members of a bill team are really the people to speak to on timings, when you can expect amendments to be published and so on. Civil servants should always be a point of contact when you are trying to learn more.

Look to utilize original source materials for the policy. You need to know where the policy has come from if you are to impact on it in any substantive way. Be prepared to look at the original report, eg a think tank report, or the Green or White paper. This approach can often provide a good list of those to involve in your campaign – did they contribute to the original paper, can you gain an understanding of where they are coming from by their initial submission to a Green Paper. This is especially important when trying to know more about those who may oppose you – only by looking at their position can you hope to be able to argue against them. Alternatively, this method can also help to identify potential allies for a campaign; you may already have supporters you can involve. Do not forget that many of these resources are available online and if they are not on a government website then they could be on the organization's own website.

Once you understand the government's position, you need to ask yourself the questions that government will ask. This will be all important if you are to succeed. If you have not thought about the government's needs and concerns then your chances of success are limited. Typical government concerns may be:

- timings;
- impact on the economy;
- cost implications;
- the popularity of your issue;
- clashes with the policies between departments.

After this research, you now know what the government's position is and can anticipate how it will react to your issue. You will also know the counter arguments you will face and have details of potential supporters. Again those involved in public affairs need to understand the policy process to advise on the framing of the arguments with government. They may vary if you are getting involved during a Green Paper but if the government has already outlined its preferred option in a White Paper then you need to frame your argument in a different manner.

We have used the example of a government above but the basic procedures remain the same whether you are lobbying a regulator, an opposition party, a business group or an NGO.

So overall:

- understand your issue;
- research the background;
- devise a solution;
- know where the issue is in the policymaking process;
- understand the position of those you are lobbying;
- ask yourself the questions that others will ask and be able to answer them;
- identify opponents and allies.

Once you have this information you are in a position to frame the argument in the briefing paper.

BUILDING THE EVIDENCE

Be prepared to know that your word may not be enough. Especially if you are arguing from a corporate position then you will hear cries of 'you would say that, wouldn't you?' Many may believe that you are simply trying to defend your own commercial position and that you only have your own best interests at heart.

When faced with this reaction you need to be able to provide evidence and also be able to show either that you are not the only ones taking this position, or that the impact of the policy will extend far beyond your own company.

You may well require some independent evidence. This can come from a number of sources:

- experts in the field prepared to extol the virtues of your position and back up your argument;
- already existing academic reports;
- press reports and comments printed elsewhere.

Yet, again, these may be insufficient. In many cases you should look to develop your arguments and give additional gravitas by working alongside an independent third party organization, such as a:

- think tank;
- economic consultancy;
- business school;
- academic department/specialist researcher;
- polling organization.

When selecting your preferred partner in this work then you need to take note of the following considerations:

- Does the partner reflect your own values? The partner should not clash with the principles of your organization, ie their aims or position being completely contradictory to your own.
- The partner should not damage your own reputation – check the background to the partner to ensure that they have not done work in the past that could cause you embarrassment or that may become more of a story than your own research.
- The partner should be recognized as a thought leader – it should be led by those with intellect and political understanding who have a good standing.
- The partner should be able to help you develop your ideas and forward them to appropriate audiences.
- Check the track record of the proposed partner.

At the end of the day, you will be working with a partner organization with the aim of providing independent verification for your position. Be sure to:

- get the brief right – when designing the research be sure to discuss your aims and objections and ensure that it is intellectually rigorous;
- be clear in the type of report you expect the partner to produce – its format, scope etc;
- be clear from the outset if the partner is in a position to help you deliver the report to your audiences;
- check on the costs – there will be budget implications for the work;
- understand if their approach resonates with the audience you are looking to influence.

There are a whole range of organizations that you may wish to consider working alongside. Below are short profiles of a number of these. It should be stressed that this is not an exhaustive list, is in alphabetical order only and the descriptions are those supplied by the organizations themselves.

THINK TANKS

The Adam Smith Institute

The UK's leading innovator of free-market policies. Named after the great Scottish economist and author of *The Wealth of Nations*, its guiding principles are free markets and a free society. It researches practical ways to inject choice and competition into public services, extend personal freedom, reduce taxes, prune back regulation, and cut government waste (www.adamsmith.org/).

The Centre for Reform

An independent, free-thinking forum for new ideas and progressive debate. It is a meeting point for people concerned about the world we live in but disillusioned with today's political solutions. It provides opportunities for people and organizations to come together and consider key issues; an alternative entry-point into the political process through ideas and debate; an opportunity to shape the future of politics through new thinking (www.cfr.org.uk/).

The Centre for European Reform

A think tank devoted to improving the quality of the debate on the future of the European Union. It is a forum for people with ideas to discuss the many political, economic and social challenges facing Europe. Based in London, the CER is a European think tank that seeks to work with similar bodies in other European countries, in North America and elsewhere in the world (www.cer.org.uk/).

Demos

A greenhouse for new ideas that can improve the quality of our lives. As an independent think tank, its aim is to create an open resource of knowledge and learning that operates beyond traditional parties, identities and disciplines. Demos connects to an international network of people changing politics (www.demos.co.uk/).

The Fabian Society

Has played a central role for more than a century in the development of political ideas and public policy on the left of centre. The Society's programme aims to explore the political ideas and the policy reforms that will define progressive politics in the new century. It is unique among think tanks in being a democratically-constituted membership organization and affiliated to the Labour Party (www.fabian-society.org.uk/int.asp).

ippr

The UK's leading progressive think tank. Through its well-researched and clearly argued policy analysis, reports and publications, its strong networks in government, academia and the corporate and voluntary sectors and high media profile, it plays a vital role in maintaining the momentum of progressive thought (www.ippr.org.uk/home/).

New Economics Foundation (NEF)

An independent 'think-and-do' tank that inspires and demonstrates real economic well-being. It aims to improve quality of life by promoting innovative solutions that challenge mainstream thinking on economic, environment and social issues. It works in partnership and puts people and the planet first (www.neweconomics.org/gen/).

Policy Exchange

An independent think tank whose mission is to develop and promote new policy ideas that will foster a free society based on strong communities, personal freedom, limited government, national self-confidence and an enterprise culture (www.policyexchange.org.uk/).

Social Market Foundation

Established in 1989 to provide a source of innovative economic and social policy ideas. Steering an independent course between political parties and conflicting ideologies, the SMF has been an influential voice in recent health, education, welfare and pensions policy reform. Its current work reflects a commitment to understanding how individuals, society and the state can work together to achieve the common goal of creating a just and free society (www.smf.co.uk/site/smf/).

Tom Bentley, Director, Demos

Appreciating the wider context in which policymakers operate is crucial in grasping how policies are formulated. The policy options they might contemplate at any given moment emerge from an increasingly complex environment shaped by the public, the media and many other organizations. In contrast to a decade ago, policymakers are far more likely to be amenable to an open and collaborative approach to policy formulation that has involved the active engagement of stakeholders from an early stage. Very often new policy development begins with discussion of a broad idea, often without detail or cost attached, which acquires momentum partly because it has been tested by widespread debate and consultation.

Equally, it is necessary to appreciate the importance that decision-makers attach to grounding policy prescriptions in practical experience. The increasing focus in government on 'policy into practice' means that proposals for change need to be grounded as far as possible in real world examples and to be integrated with hard edged strategies for implementation.

ECONOMIC CONSULTANCIES

There are a number of specialist economic consultancies available, and those below are merely a small selection. For instance, other accountancy firms such as PricewaterhouseCoopers also have a consultancy arm.

Centre for Economics and Business Research

An independent consultancy with a reputation for sound business advice based on thorough and insightful research. Since 1992, CEBR has been at the forefront of business and public interest research. It provides analysis, forecasts and strategic advice to companies of all sizes, financial institutions, government departments and agencies, trade bodies and the European Commission (www.cebr.com).

Ernst and Young

Helps companies in businesses across all industries deal with a broad range of business issues. It provides a range of services, including accounting and auditing, tax reporting and operations, tax advisory, business risk services, technology and security risk services, transaction advisory, and human capital services (www.ey.com/global/content.nsf/International/Home).

KPMG

A global network of professional services firms providing audit, tax and advisory services. It operates in 148 countries and has around 6,500 partners, 70,000 client service professionals, and 17,000 administration and support staff working in member firms around the world. It aims to provide clients with a globally consistent set of multidisciplinary financial and accounting services, based on deep industry knowledge (www.kpmg.com/index.asp).

BUSINESS SCHOOLS

There are a number of business schools available to you, and those listed below are merely a small selection. For instance, other universities such as Leeds Metropolitan University, Cranfield University and Henley Management College, also have excellent business schools.

Cass

Is part of City University and has an international perspective. An environment created for learning, not teaching. A place where students, academics, industry experts, business leaders and policymakers can share ideas, and enrich each other's thinking. Whatever you experience, Cass say that you will find an openness, energy and intelligence that mark out its staff, students, alumni and partners (www.cass.city.ac.uk).

London Business School

Is consistently ranked as one of the top business schools in the world, and is committed to becoming the pre-eminent global business school. Theirs is an expanding and international community of 100-plus world-renowned faculty, 23,000 international alumni, over 1,000 culturally diverse graduate students and 6,000 executive education participants a year (www.london.edu).

POLLING ORGANIZATIONS

Gallup

Has studied human nature and behaviour for more than 70 years. Gallup employs many of the world's leading scientists in management, economics, psychology and sociology. Gallup performance management systems help organizations increase customer engagement and maximize employee productivity through measurement tools, coursework and strategic advisory services (www.gallup.com).

MORI

Was founded in 1969 and is one of Britain's fastest growing market and public opinion research agencies. It provides a full range of quantitative and qualitative research services, working with hundreds of clients in both the private and public sectors. MORI embraces both traditional and technologically advanced research methods (www.mori.com).

YouGov

A research company using online panels to provide research for public policy, market research, and stakeholder consultation. YouGov has a track record as the UK's most accurate pollster. In all five of the YouGov polls where data could be compared to actual outcomes, they were within one per cent of the actual result (www.yougov.com).

Opinion Leader Research

Specializes in understanding an organization's reputation and the drivers of that reputation, through engaging with the audiences that matter – from senior decision-makers through to those that shape and mould opinions in their own peer groups. They have developed innovative thinking on how influence and communications work in society, and work with organizations to meet the growing demand for involvement and interaction (www.opinionleader.co.uk/).

Internationally, a number of other bodies are available to work with. For instance, there are a huge number of think tanks in the US and in individual European member states. Some of the most respected business schools are in the US. Do not hesitate to look abroad for partners, especially if you are lobbying in Brussels.

BUILDING SUPPORT

Once your report has been developed, researched and written then it is time to employ it as part of your public affairs campaign. This can take a number of forms but should include:

- Briefing paper – use the evidence in your briefing paper.
- Opinion former meetings – as a first port of call your research should be presented to key opinion formers. Who these are will vary upon the nature of the campaign and the stage that it is at. However, a meeting with the key civil servant, minister or main political supporter would be a useful starting point.
- Media relations – aim to launch the report in the press as this can make a splash and help to apply pressure on your key audiences. You may want to offer an 'exclusive' to an influential outlet (press or broadcast) or issue a press release more generally to gain as much coverage as possible but probably in less detail.

Graeme Trayner, Director, Opinion Leader Research

Effective research is about understanding current views and attitudes, and pinpointing what can change opinions. That's why it needs to be at the heart of any public affairs strategy.

Indeed, research should guide your strategy, rather than just being viewed as a dry measurement tool. Through the use of opinion surveys and qualitative research, public affairs practitioners can spot opportunities and threats, discover the messages that resonate, and identify the strategies that can win.

In this sense, practitioners need to follow the lead of their counterparts in frontline politics, and use research to help influence decision-making. As Reagan advisor Ed Rollins said, trying to run a campaign 'without polling is like flying an airplane without instruments.' And that is as true for the boardroom as it is for the war room.

As part of your campaign you should also look to build support for your position among third party organizations. Potential supporters will vary depending on the sector and the nature of the campaign. However, the general rule is the more support the better. The more you can clearly show that you are not a lone voice but are instead part of a group then the chances of success will be increased.

The development of a network of 'friends' in advance of any campaign is always to be encouraged as this makes life a lot easier if an issue arises. In the real world this is not always the case and part of the role of a public affairs professional is to help in the identification of potential allies and to help attract them to the cause. Each potential ally will come at the issue from a slightly different perspective and this needs to be recognized in any approach to maximize the possibility of involvement. Be prepared to identify the allies, understand where they are coming from, address any issues they have and gain their support in a way that can be used in the campaign, ie publicly if at all possible.

You may need to establish contact with organizations or competitors who have previously been considered opponents. However, to maximize the chances of success these attitudes should be put to one side so that the group becomes as deep and wide as possible.

Potential allies may come from:

- Interest groups – it is possible that some existing groups may be supportive.
- Trade bodies – the representative body for the industry may become involved if a number of member organizations feel strongly. Such bodies often have good links in government and political circles and a network of political friends who can forward your cause. Bodies that represent a number of organizations carry additional weight as they are seen not be fighting the corner of only one company but a whole industry, sector or representative group.
- Competitors – on certain issues it may be that competitors have more in common than usual. It is still possible to fight competitively even though the same platform is shared.
- Celebrities – the use of celebrities is often considered to be more for those involved in PR. However, a celebrity endorsement can be used in a public affairs campaign to add profile and help secure useful press coverage. A celebrity endorsement, or that of any other third party organization, can be a clear demonstration that your position has wide support.
- Politicians – if the campaign is not a strictly party political one, then you can aim to secure the support of politicians or maybe former politicians whose names remain known to the general public.

Each of these audiences may want particular angles from the campaign and want to know different information, have differing questions. The importance of understanding the needs of your audiences is explored in more detail in the chapter on stakeholder relations. At this stage it needs to be understood that the way in which you approach potential allies needs to reflect their own position and demonstrate a clear awareness of their needs and requirements. Similarly, when working with outside bodies be sure that no one from among your third party supporters is likely to damage your reputation. Celebrity endorsements may be useful but if they are likely to utter controversial statements then their support may do more harm than good.

In the quest to build support for your issue and campaign, profile is important. Media relations are discussed in a separate chapter and should be a fundamental element. However, other profile building and support gathering strategies are available:

- Events – a large set piece conference can bring together the audiences you are trying to work with. Themed around your issue, you could invite your audiences to hear a number of speakers and be involved in a discussion on the topic. Such events can also be smaller in scale, eg a breakfast or lunchtime seminar. A 'for' versus 'against' speaker arrangement is the simplest form of such an event.
- Online debates – increasingly debates take place online and encourage input from a range of contributors. The initial starting point for the debate may be a paper you have produced or a media report on the issue.
- A website – a must for any campaign is the establishment of a website. The site should provide those with an interest with details of your arguments, key messages etc. In addition, it should:
  - allow for feedback, through a dedicated web address;
  - become a depository for media coverage that people can view;
  - detail any support given, the names of supporters, quotes from debates or media pieces;
  - answer any questions people may have, possibly in a 'Question & Answer' section;
  - perhaps allow online debate as part of the site, on a message board.

Those involved in public affairs should not adopt a 'silo mentality' and need to look for ideas and support wherever they can get it from. There is nothing worse than to rule out a possible source of support simply because you do not understand it yourself or feel that it belongs to a different part of the PR rubric. Be prepared to look for assistance from other areas of PR in helping you to sell your messages, gain support and possibly endorsements. Consider the role that the following can play:

- Designers – can they make your website look better, or assist in the production of a high-quality leaflet aimed at your audience?

- Advertisers – can a well-placed advert help to build support and what form should that advert take?

In a more strictly political setting, the conferences held by each of the parties can play a useful role in gaining political profile and support for your campaign. The party conferences are a mainstay of public affairs activity but they have to be considered more carefully nowadays so that the most is made of the opportunities they present. Each of the political parties holds a main conference in September or October each year. Traditionally these were held in seaside towns in years gone by to allow people to enjoy a week away from the cities. In addition, there are also spring conferences but these are less important in terms of policymaking and are less well attended. For parties such as the Labour Party there are also a series of other conferences, for instance for women or councillors. Depending on the nature of the party, the conferences play a role in their policymaking procedures and represent the one time of year when the party comes together as a whole.

For those involved in public affairs, attendance at the party conferences is an essential part of the job. Spending a week with each party assists in the process of understanding how the party works, what the opinions are of members and activists and how policy is built. The party conference season is also an excellent time to network and build contacts. The challenge is, however, how to make the most of the party conferences when involved in campaigning. There are a number of options open:

- Attendance – for those involved in the campaign, going to the party conferences may help to develop the arguments after hearing from a variety of audiences but may also provide opportunities to hear or meet those making the decision.
- Fringe events – fringe events take place throughout all the party conferences and also those for other organizations, for instance trade unions. Many hundreds take place during the week of a party conference on a whole range of issues, some controversial, others not. For those involved in a campaign, organizing and holding a fringe meeting offers the opportunity of ensuring that the issue is heard and raised during the conference. This is, however, not enough; you have to make sure that you are able to attract the right calibre of speakers and also a sufficiently large audience that is, of course, partly dependent on the quality of speakers. A fringe event takes a lot of organizing but a brief checklist would include:
  - Book an appropriate room for the event (think about being close to the main conference call, when the leaders' speech will take place, best to hold it at lunchtime or in the evening). Be warned, to secure

  a good venue you may have to book around a year in advance of the conference.
  - Decide on your topic and frame the title/question in a way that will attract speakers and an audience. Consider which title sounds best from these two on the same issue: 'Maternity rights: the future' or 'The End of Working Mothers?'
  - Invite your speakers and get the balance right, for instance if you are holding a debate make sure you generate a for/against debate. A government minister or similar high-profile speaker is essential if you are to make any impact.
  - Consider inviting those audiences you are trying to communicate with as part of your campaign with letters nearer the event.
  - Check on the needs of speakers, for instance do they need security passes? As a more general point, anyone attending a party conference needs to obtain a pass from the relevant party. There are different types available and the costs vary but be sure to check the application deadlines.
  - Each of the parties publishes a listings of fringe events taking place during the conference and it is essential that your event is listed. Again there are deadlines to meet and if you are not listed then you are really limiting your chances of a good turnout.
  - Order appropriate refreshments, food and drink. A good selection can help attract an audience and keep them in the room!
  - Order appropriate supporting materials, for instance stands, brochures, banners etc. You may also need computing equipment, projectors or microphones.
  - Double check EVERYTHING!
- Dinners/breakfasts – rather than fringe events that look to encourage delegates and others to attend, you may prefer a more specialist briefing during the conference week. A breakfast or dinner can enable you to invite a speaker plus selected invitees.
- Speaking opportunities – it may be that your organization is asked to speak at someone else's fringe event. The relevant merits of taking part will have to be considered on a case by case basis; however, it may provide an opportunity to raise your own issue.
- Corporate events – each of the parties nowadays holds events especially geared towards the needs of the corporate sector. These events offer the opportunity to hear from and possibly meet those at the top of the party, eg ministers or key spokespersons. The events, often held over one or two days, are based on a series of seminars that allow for interaction with attendees, often include good seats for the leader's speech (the highlight of the conference) and a seat at the main conference dinner. Attendance can be very useful but costs are high.

- Exhibitions – exhibition stands are located around the main conference hall and these are taken by many types of businesses, trade unions, specialist campaigns, NGOs etc all hoping to catch the eye of MPs and also raise the profile of their issues.
- Sponsorship – all of the political parties are very proficient at offering sponsorship opportunities throughout their conference week. Opportunities include guides, badges, even the steps at the conference venue! There is no space that cannot be sponsored at the modern party conference except the main stage area from which speeches are made and that is the subject of the media spotlight. You can also take a table at the main gala dinner, which is often considered one of the highlights of the conference away from the main floor; again the cost is very high.
- Sponsoring a party event – the parties also organize their own events during the conference that include, for instance, drinks receptions for foreign ambassadors or the party's local councillors.
- Advertising in the town where the conference is taking place – this has become more popular in recent years with banners and advertising space taken during the conference week.

Do not forget that bodies that you work with, competitors and others, may also hold their own events during the conferences that you could consider attending. These can provide useful intelligence for your own campaign and are often good benchmarks if you are considering doing your own event in future.

Outside the conference, all of the political parties also hold specialized events or dinners during the course of a year, eg for lawyers or councillors. All three main parties also now encourage more open engagement with business and other organizations and have their own business liaison organizations. Membership of these organizations provides invitations to seminars on a range of topics addressed by senior people from the party and for reasonable informal interaction and networking. In their own words:

- The Conservative Party Enterprise Forum
  - Aims to build a network of communication between the Conservative Party and business leaders, is one of the pioneers of bringing business and party politics together. Only by creating a structured environment where the free flow of ideas can be heard can a true representation be achieved. The Enterprise Forum provides an independent middle ground where the views of business can be those of the Party (www.enterprise-forum.co.uk).

- Labour Party Industry Forum
  - Creates dialogue between business and government in order to develop better policy. Its member organizations are mostly drawn from large and medium sized enterprises, including trade bodies, from most sectors of UK business. Activities of the Industry Forum, such as ministerial meetings, working groups, seminars and conferences, take place in London, other parts of the UK and Europe. The Industry Forum undertakes research and activities with the aim of improving policies and practices that affect UK business. Recent and ongoing studies include reforming the civil service, improving productivity, the needs of creative industries, and better understanding and management of risk (www.industry-forum.org/index.php).
- The Liberal Democrat Business Forum
  - Aims to provide a two-way exchange mechanism between business and industry on the one hand, and the DTI, Treasury and other relevant parliamentary teams on the other. An effective dialogue between these two groups is vital in order for the Party to take account of the concerns of business when developing policy and to inform the business community of the Party's views (www.inbusiness.libdems.org.uk/pages/Questions.html).

An important consideration when spending money at any party event is that the money you spend may be listed as a 'donation' to the party under the terms of the Political Parties, Elections and Referendums Act (2000). This may mean that you have some reputation-related issues to consider and may also mean that you get involved with a number of the political parties, not just the one in government.

CONCLUSION

One of the most important parts in building and maintaining a campaign is that you must never hesitate to revisit your ideas and strategy papers and make alterations if necessary. If the policy setting alters or new comments are made then incorporate them. You will also need to stay alert to new issues as they arise and consider how they impact on your position. At the same time, however, there must remain a consistency of core messages across all your audiences and the mediums through which you are communicating. If people think that you are merely being expedient then you will never get anywhere.

The details in this chapter have been a guide to conducting a campaign with an assumed outcome being achieved. But many campaigns are ongoing. If one set of objectives is achieved then the campaign is reassessed, a new set of objectives decided, the good work undertaken to date built upon and developed, and work continues. For instance, if the government were to accept your argument that research money should be awarded to a new form of energy generation then the campaign may be developed to set targets that a certain percentage of electricity generated should come from the new method, or that three new plants should be built in the UK. Campaigns grow and develop over time and so, therefore, should the public affairs strategy.

In summary, there are a number of practical steps in developing an issues-led campaign:

- Understand your issue and the policymaking setting – you cannot develop a campaign without knowing what you want to alter and how.
- Build the evidence – never assume that people will just take your word for it, get outside help if necessary.
- Build support – who might offer their support?
- Develop an online presence – people use the web as a source of information and they need to be able to find out about you.
- Build a profile – think about organizing an event, look through the political calendar for opportunities, think creatively about how you can get people to know about the campaign.
- Where do you go from here? If you achieve your desired outcome, is that the end of the story? What can you do next?

Simon Lewis, Group Corporate Affairs Director, Vodafone Group

It is important to think of public policy and public affairs as an iceberg above and below the waterline. On the surface is the public face of political life, elections, the House of Commons and the day to day business of parliamentary activity. Below the surface is where the public policy debate begins, in the think tanks and the policy networks. When the ideas reach the surface the ability to influence may be limited. So my 'top tip' is to ensure that in any public affairs or public policy programme, you are following closely the output from and developments in think tanks and policy networks. Being close to the emerging ideas can be invaluable if and when they reach the stage of legislation.

**Katherine Bennett OBE MIPR,
Head of Government Affairs, Airbus UK**

My tried and tested premise for establishing good government relations contacts really holds true for creating or developing any kind of new relationship.

What makes them tick (background, interests etc)?

Prepare a good opening line in order to create an association between, for example, your connection with a constituency. This goes back to the old adage you learn in presentation skills training, ie make them feel good about themselves.

Provide succinct, relevant information about the company or organization you represent.

Ask them questions about their immediate area of interest, ie what is in their 'in tray'? Raise your topic, bearing in mind there is nothing worse than someone launching into their issue without taking note of the environment around them or the initial body language of the recipient of the message.

Finally, a tip I learned from a former parliamentarian I worked with. An immediate personal handwritten note, e-mail or even text to say thanks can go a long way.

Graham McMillan, Head of Public Affairs, Fishburn Hedges

Make friends before you need them. If you need help from your friends, make sure you have some.

Build long term credibility. Strong relationships are based on years of hard work with key policymakers where you continually show you can be relied on for good analysis and information, and honest opinions that take account of broader public interest.

Sort out your messages. Don't just whinge. Try to be constructive if possible and frame your case in a way that appeals to the broader long term aims of government. Think carefully about what it is you want policymakers and legislators to do. Test your arguments to check that they hold water.

Build a coalition where possible and secure third party endorsement: assertion from you alone is rarely enough. You need the support of others and your arguments need to be backed up by authoritative independent information and research where possible.

Try to be imaginative. You are competing for share of voice with many other organizations. Is there a way you can approach the issue that will offer fresh insight? Is there a way you can bring it alive by showing policymakers first hand what you mean?

2001 CENSUS PUBLICITY CAMPAIGN IN SCOTLAND

The objective of the publicity campaign, run by Craig Lindsay Communications with Cunningham & Co, for the 2001 Census of population in Scotland – run separately from campaigns for England, Wales and Northern Ireland – was to inform all households that they would receive a census form before 29 April 2001 and that they had a legal duty to complete and return the form.

It was also necessary to explain why the census was so important and special efforts were made to reach people in known problem groups who were historically reluctant to provide the personal information required.

The aims of the media strategy were:

- to raise awareness of the census among the 5.5 million population of Scotland;
- to inform people why the census was so important to them personally;
- to assure people the census was totally impartial, non-political and confidential;
- to assure people the census was being run by a thoroughly professional organization with an impeccable record;
- to persuade people to return completed census forms in good time;
- to persuade people that the census was not government 'prying' and personal details would be kept secret.

With the objectives set it was important that the key messages developed were adapted and developed to inform particular groups of people. The messages included:

- results are vital to improving Scotland;
- first census under a Scottish parliament, and a 'landmark' census;
- impartiality;
- strict confidentiality;
- legal duty to complete the census form;
- help with filling in the census form available to those who need it.

The campaign was based on the following:

- An extensive PR programme of news releases and briefings for editors was devised. Contacts were made in print media as diverse as church magazines and ethnic minority newsletters. In addition, a comprehensive, three-stage, paid-for advertising campaign was developed in conjunction with an agency normally engaged on Scottish Executive publicity, and bookings were made in national, regional and local print and broadcast media.

- Advertisements appeared first in early March 2001, six weeks before Census Day. However, the 'drip feed' issue of PR news releases to mark milestones in the organization of the census began much earlier, in October 2000, to allow editors and journalists to get to know their local census contacts.
- A key contributing factor to the excellent editorial support from the Scottish regional media was the series of personal briefings by the Registrar General for editors of the three principal newspaper groups in Scotland and many other individual editors and journalists. These face-to-face meetings added a personal touch that engendered continual local coverage of census activities and ensured readers were thoroughly familiar with the word 'census' long before 29 April 2001.

All media pack content offered to journalists was written to be 'sub-friendly' and ready to be used easily and quickly by them. The pack contained seven news releases and a copy of the Census Launch Brief; a specimen census form; a general information leaflet on the census in Scotland; a leaflet on language identification cards and a general information leaflet on how the census results will be used. Visual material was confined to copies of old census records of famous Scots, and photographs of the Registrar General. They made use of a 40ft by 20ft colour map of Scotland by standing each of the 22 Census Area Managers on their 'patch' and issuing group and individual pictures to the media.

The programme really benefited from the four leaders of the main political parties in Scotland, including the First Minister and Deputy First Minister, giving their public and joint support to the census at the official publicity campaign launch ceremony in March 2001.

The campaign was very effective – all 8,000 field staff found everyone contacted at 2.2 million homes was well aware of the event, and more than 90 per cent of the 150,000 callers to the telephone help lines wanted to know when their form was going to be delivered. The results of the editorial coverage generated, if measured by using advertising equivalents, during the period from the launch on 8 March until Census Day on 29 April, amounted to approximately £110,000.

This programme demonstrates the importance of tailoring messages to secure a successful outcome and the positive role that political support can play.

5

Stakeholder relations

No organization, group or business develops, exists and operates in a vacuum. Organizations are inextricable from the society, economy, political system and physical environment in which they are based. These same organizations also impact on, contribute to and in the worst cases detract from, the societies, economies, political systems and physical environments in a large number of ways.

Not too many years ago it was thought that the only ones who really had a stake in a company were its owners or shareholders. However, there is now a more general acceptance that the range of those with a stake is much wider. They range from the primary interest groups – employees, clients, shareholders – to groups more disconnected from the day to day running of an organization – the community in which it is based, political representatives and the general public.

For those in public affairs this has meant a realization that there are a wide number of audiences that need to be reached. In addition, communicating with these audiences can also provide opportunities but they need to be managed effectively. A key element of any public affairs, or indeed broader corporate communications strategy, must now include the efficient management of all stakeholder relationships.

The principles of identification and communication with stakeholders outlined in this chapter are common to all types of organizations, not just commercial ones. All organizations have a multitude of different formal or informal groups that hold a stake or an interest in what the organization does.

THE VALUE OF STAKEHOLDERS

Stakeholders are any individual or group that, directly or indirectly, affect or are affected by the operations of your organization. They can be external or internal. More specifically, stakeholders can positively or negatively influence an organization's ability to develop and thrive, in the long term and also more immediately. Stakeholders can potentially be an organization's most significant, but under-used, asset. They must not be taken for granted however. It is important to take the time to understand, manage and develop those relationships in the 'good times', when things are going well and there may be no threats of any type on the horizon. Stakeholder relationships have positive value in their own right by increasing mutual understanding and, for instance, assisting in the identification of commercial opportunities or boosting organizational efficiency.

Strong relationships with stakeholders are equally crucial during the 'bad times', perhaps when change is occurring or when policy or commercial threats emerge. If properly mobilized, stakeholders can be powerful advocates for, and defenders of, an organization's interests.

Stakeholders provide organizations with the 'on the ground' support that they need, helping to protect and promote. The value is, however, often intangible and therefore hard to quantify. At a minimum, they are a part of good business practice, protecting and enhancing an organization's reputation, and managing and communicating the impact of an organization on the society in which it operates. By communicating with stakeholders early and frequently, an organization ensures that they fully understand its objectives and the benefits it delivers. This in turn means the stakeholders can be mobilized to support the organization actively, when necessary. Building these relationships provides a reservoir of goodwill that can be drawn upon when challenges and difficulties arise. In terms of contribution to the 'bottom-line', more positively, the opening of new channels and the development of relationships can bring fresh insights, opportunities and add value that an organization might not otherwise be able to access.

The principles of a successful stakeholder relations strategy are broadly similar to those of lobbying and public affairs campaigns more generally. Stakeholders or audiences must be identified, and effective communications must be tailored to the individual requirements of those stakeholders. An organization must have a clear understanding of who its stakeholders are, their motivations and interests, their importance on any given issue, and their current perceptions, expectations and requirements of an organization.

This chapter examines the importance of identifying, understanding and communicating with your organization's stakeholders.

IDENTIFY YOUR STAKEHOLDERS

Who are your stakeholders? They range from those with the most direct stake in your organization – your employees, customers and financial investors – to those whose stake is more removed – your political representatives, and the institutions that shape public policy in your area. Your stakeholders will vary depending on the type of your organization, sector, size and structure.

Some of your stakeholders will be obvious as they are directly related to the primary purpose or activities of the organization, whereas others will be more indirect but equally important. The first stage in a programme of stakeholder relations should be to identify or 'map' your stakeholders. To do this requires a very good understanding of not only the organization itself and its sector but also factors such as where your locations are (head office, factories etc), and which other companies or organizations with which you have contact or existing relations.

Common types of stakeholder are outlined below.

Direct stakeholders:

- employees (and their families and friends);
- members;
- customers;
- clients;
- suppliers and other contractors/service providers (and, more indirectly, their suppliers in turn).

Financial stakeholders:

- shareholders and investors – both institutional and individuals;
- other financial stakeholders – providers of finance, guarantors, trustees etc;
- business partners.

Public stakeholders:

- Political representatives – national, regional and local. Also, both geographical and sectoral political representatives – both the local Member of Parliament and the relevant Department of Trade and Industry Minister, if the organization concerned was a manufacturer, for instance:
  - 'public' policymaking communities – government departments and agencies;
  - 'private' policymaking communities – think tanks and academia;
  - regulatory bodies – both public and self-regulatory organizations.

Representative stakeholders:

- trade unions;
- membership and representative organizations – trade associations, federations, etc;
- broader representative groups – the CBI, the Institute of Directors, Chambers of Commerce etc;
- interest groups – non-governmental organizations and campaign groups. These can be local, national or, increasingly, international.

Geographical stakeholders:

- Local, regional and national communities.

Effective stakeholders; related to the organization:

- 'emotional' communities – friends, families, supporters and fans;
- alumni and retirees;
- peers – both sectoral (your competitors) and geographic (other local businesses or organizations).

Media:

- local, regional, national and trade;
- broadcast, print and new media;
- analysts and commentators.

And the general public!

The categories and types outlined above are indicative rather than exhaustive. New stakeholders will arise all the time as your organization grows and develops. For instance, if a new product comes to market then you will have a new set of stakeholders or if you open a new office then again your list of stakeholders grows. Furthermore, stakeholder groups cannot be regarded in isolation; few of the categories are discrete or mutually exclusive. Stakeholder groups can be closely interlinked; they will frequently overlap in membership and have enormous potential to influence each other. The most obvious example being that your employees may also be your customers.

Perhaps more than any other single stakeholder group, especially for large-scale employers, employees are crucial stakeholders. They are an organization's social grounding in the communities in which it is based. Moreover, they can be an important conduit into other stakeholder groups, most importantly political stakeholders, the media and trade unions. Giving an organization's employees the tools and will to be ambassadors or advocates for an organization will add value. Constant engagement and dialogue is a priority with employees perhaps above all other groups.

Technology has also changed the nature and scale of stakeholder groups with geographic proximity or commonality of culture no longer a constraint. Of course, this is common in all areas of life, not just stakeholder relations. As the president of the US Public Affairs Council, Doug Pinkham, remarked, 'The internet is changing the way the media report on political issues, the way the government interacts with the public, the way corporations communicate with their stakeholders and the balance of power between interest-groups.'

Stakeholders are not constant or fixed; they evolve, expand, contract and sometimes disappear altogether. In short, an organization's potential stakeholders are wide-ranging and the challenge for any organization is to understand these stakeholders, prioritize the most important ones on any particular issue, and to reach them in the most effective way.

UNDERSTANDING YOUR STAKEHOLDERS

Once you have identified who your stakeholders are, you need to map them. To do this you must work out their relative levels of power, influence and interest and prioritize them. Relative priority will of course depend on the nature of the particular issue (threat or opportunity) facing your organization, or whether you are conducting general communications with all your key stakeholders. For the sake of simplicity, the rest of this chapter assumes that there is a particular issue in question.

You must develop a good understanding of the most important stakeholders so you know how they are likely to respond to particular issues and how active they would be prepared to be. Prioritize your stakeholders by their power, influence and interest – from the important/active/effective to the unimportant/inactive/ineffective. Some may have the power to block or advance your organization's case. Some may be interested, some may not. Some can be made to be interested. The key information you need to know about your stakeholders is as follows:

- What are the stakeholders' primary motivations? What else motivates them?
- What financial, physical, social or emotional interests do the stakeholders have in your work or this issue? Are these positive or negative interests? What can be done to raise (or indeed lower) their interest?
- What are the stakeholders' current perceptions of your organization? Are these accurate perceptions?
- What are the stakeholders' current perceptions of the issue in question? Have they adopted a public position on the issue? Are their current perceptions based on good information?
- Who or what influences the stakeholders' perceptions? Who influences their perceptions of your organization? Should you also be communicating with those influencers?
- Who else do those stakeholders influence? Should you be communicating with those that they influence directly?
- What information do the stakeholders need from you? What information should they have? What is the best means of communication to deliver this information?
- If the stakeholders are positive, what can they most effectively do for you? What is their appetite for direct involvement? What role do you want them to play?
- What, if anything, can you do to bolster the stakeholders' support?
- If the stakeholders are not positive, what, if anything, will win them round?
- If it is not possible to win the stakeholders round, how can their opposition be managed or mitigated? Can they be isolated?
- How important are the stakeholders to your argument?

The answers to the questions above are central to the development of your stakeholder communications strategy. They help you to prioritize your stakeholders and understand what you need to do to reach them effectively.

In short, after identifying your stakeholders, you must understand whether they are potential advocates, supporters, neutrals, critics, or blockers. Advocates are strong supporters prepared to be active and take up your case, either in public or behind the scenes. Your supporters are just that, but may not be as prepared to take as active a role as your advocates in articulating their support. Neutrals can either be worked around or won over, if you have a particularly strong case. The view of a neutral can be especially powerful if it can, by force of argument and appropriate communication, be brought to bear on your behalf. Critics will position themselves against you but will not be as active in their opposition as blockers will be. Both would almost always have a vested interest against your case; however, this can often be used to isolate their opposition. You will have to make a judgement in any given scenario about how much time and effort you must spend in communicating with these groups and with what objective. It will be important to remember that your opponents will rarely be passive and you will have to develop an understanding of the arguments pitched against you and be prepared to rebut and respond as necessary to keep on the front foot.

ENGAGING YOUR STAKEHOLDERS

Once you understand what you need from each stakeholder and what role you want them to play you need to identify the messages you need to communicate to them and the actions that are necessary to do this. What do you need to do to keep your best supporters engaged and on board? How do you neutralize the opposition of sceptics? Where do you need the active support of stakeholders who are not currently interested in what you are doing? What can you do to engage with them and raise their level of interest? Most importantly, you must consider how what you are trying to achieve will impact on them.

Your broad messages to all stakeholders must be consistent and coordinated, and certainly never contradictory. Indeed, organizations with the strongest reputations communicate a consistent and coherent set of principles across all stakeholder groups. However, your messages must also be tailored to each stakeholder, bearing in mind the answers to the questions outlined above. What are the messages that will carry the most resonance with each audience? What shows the benefit of what you are trying to achieve in the most tangible possible way? What do you want them to do specifically? Communication must never be one way and you also need to consider what is required to enable a dialogue with your stakeholders.

Stakeholders can be both organizations and people. However, ultimately you are communicating with people. Consequently, you must identify the correct people within the stakeholder group to target, whilst bearing in mind that an individual's motivations may differ from his or her role within the organization. Who is the correct person in your organization to manage that relationship – should it be a technical person, a trade union member, a member of the finance team, your corporate social responsibility team, the chief executive or the chairperson? Members of the communications team will not always be the most appropriate people to own all of your stakeholder relationships. However, it will be the responsibility of the communications team to identify, audit, understand and mobilize those relationships when the time comes.

You should consider what is the most appropriate mechanism of communication with each stakeholder. Is it written or oral? Via letters, newsletters, leaflets, campaign bulletins? Through forums, focus groups, conferences, group meetings or one-on-one meetings? How much detail will be required? Would electronic communication be more effective and timely – by e-mail, the worldwide web, online discussion forums, web logs? How formal or informal should communications be? Should you communicate directly or indirectly, through the media etc?

Timescale is also essential. You should focus your resources on active/effective stakeholders first and you should implement a practical communications strategy that communicates with your priority groups as effectively as possible, delivering the correct amount of information, in the most appropriate format and with clarity about what your expectations are of your stakeholders.

Rod Cartwright, Director, Public Affairs, Hill & Knowlton; Chair, Public Affairs Committee, Public Relations Consultants Association

Public affairs all too often runs the risk of supposing that improving an organization's profile and levels of understanding is of inherent value.

Wrong. Public affairs, as with all communications, must be driven by the core priorities of the organization in question with regard to business, organization and reputation. Therefore, the first step in developing an effective public affairs strategy must be to ask:

- What are our main corporate and business priorities?
- Do politics and public policy actually affect these priorities – and if so how?
- What are our overall communications objectives?

Asking these sorts of questions is the only way to develop a workable public affairs strategy that truly reflects the corporate and communications priorities that will underpin the implementation of that strategy.

PLANNING COMMUNICATIONS

Planning can be a very political process and is a good example of how stakeholder relations can be employed to positive effect. By working with your organization's stakeholders you can show support for a planning application and bring pressure to bear on those making the decisions. To look at planning communications in detail would require another whole book but, in general terms, it can be seen as the pre-planned and strategic engagement with stakeholders. If we consider the example of the application for a new supermarket we could think of the following as stakeholders:

- employees – if there is a store already nearby;
- local residents – they may also be organized into groups;
- local businesses – they may also be organized into groups (Chambers of Commerce, trader's body etc);
- local organizations – such as pressure groups (historical societies, transport groups etc);
- politicians – at all levels (MPs and councillors) but especially those on the relevant council;
- planning committee members – those who will have the final say on the application;
- planning officers – the employees of the council who work with applicants on the detail of the application, write reports on the application and advise the planning committee;
- regional bodies – such as regional development agencies (RDAs) and government offices;
- local media – press and broadcast.

This is not an exhaustive list but it demonstrates the range and diversity of stakeholders involved. It is also clear that the motivations and positions of these groups may vary and when looking to move forward with an application you have to be able to explain it to each of them, bearing in mind that position and the questions they will want answers to. Only in this way will you be able to attract supporters and minimize opposition.

The position of each of the stakeholders will, in turn, influence the manner in which you communicate with them. For instance, an exhibition may be a good way to engage with a large number of local residents but consider the type of materials that should be available with information about the project – display boards, leaflets that can be taken away, comment cards for people to fill in etc. Briefing papers are often used to communicate with political audiences but one-to-one briefings may be appropriate as may presentations to the whole of the planning committee.

Particular attention should be paid to the local media as controversy over a planning application makes for very good news. Local media, therefore, often have a vested interest in making the most of an application and letting the two sides of the debate fight it out across the pages of the press. An applicant should be very careful about this and this means knowing how to deal with the media and being able to provide them with positive stories.

Planning law is constantly changing and engagement is an increasingly important element in the planning process. The planning authorities need to engage with their stakeholders when devising their strategies and the applicants now need to submit a Statement of Community Involvement (SCI). The statements are designed to ensure the public has access to adequate information about planning applications, has the opportunity to input into process and for developers this means that pre-application consultation will increasingly be the norm.

The government is attempting to foster a better engagement with the private sector and wants to involve communities in delivering sustainable local solutions. It recognizes that a tension exists between the local voice of objectors, who are usually in the minority, and the wider benefits that development schemes can offer, benefits that the silent majority support. The task for applicants is to engage with community at an early stage, show that the community has been involved and how the plans have changed or evolved as a result of that engagement, and succeed in encouraging some of the otherwise silent majority to be complementary about the application and act as a champion.

As a general guide to planning communications:

1. Identify friends, allies and potential opponents – all the stakeholders.
2. Engage with them as early as possible.
3. Tailor materials/engagement to the needs of your stakeholders.
4. Do not underestimate the power of the media.
5. Talk to local politicians – at all levels.
6. Keep planning officials/officers in touch with your strategy.
7. Ensure the messages are closely aligned to planning/legal arguments.
8. If your plans change be prepared to tell people.
9. Do not forget to tell audiences about how you have engaged locally.
10. When you get your result keep the engagement going – maintain your reputation by continuing stakeholder engagement.

SUMMARY

Your stakeholders are potentially one of your organization's most valuable assets. However, to take advantage of these assets any organization needs to think strategically about its communications with both internal and external stakeholders to build understanding, trust and to add value to the organization. An organization's reputation is, arguably, the sum of its relationships with its stakeholders. The stakes they hold may or may not be direct but they all play an important role in conditioning the economic, financial, social, political and physical context in which your organization is operating. These relationships will be important in both the good times, when you should invest the time and effort in identifying and understanding your key stakeholders, and the bad times, when you may need your stakeholders to advocate on your behalf.

Although regrettably this is frequently not the case, it is always recommended to have engaged with stakeholders in advance of having to call on them in, for instance, times of crisis. Just as you cannot ignore your opponents, you must not neglect your friends or take them for granted. By engaging early, you can use the opinions of influential stakeholders to inform and improve your subsequent communications with other stakeholders, and shape your campaign at an early stage. By being able to anticipate likely reactions to your messages better, you are more likely to win support. Furthermore, by communicating with stakeholders early and frequently, you can ensure that they fully understand the objectives of your organization and the benefits of what you are doing, which means that they will be far more likely to actively support you when necessary.

A communications professional should think creatively about who his or her organization's stakeholders are. You may think of your employees as stakeholders but why not think of former employees as stakeholders as well? Technology has enabled wider and new types of stakeholder communities no longer strictly constrained by geography. Stakeholders are not static, they evolve with time and technology. How do you reach these stakeholders and leverage the value they represent? Football clubs, for example, are increasingly recognizing the value of tapping directly into their supporter or stakeholder bases using technology that allows, for instance, MUTV to be beamed directly into its customers' homes.[1]

In all cases, you need a clear understanding of who your stakeholders are, their relative interests and importance on a particular issue, and their current perceptions of, and requirements of your organization, their appetite for direct involvement and what you need them to do. You also need to know how to best engage them in your project and how to best communicate with them. Be consistent but tailor your message to resonate with each stakeholder. Any practical stakeholder communications strategy must communicate with the key (important/active/effective) stakeholders as effectively and as rapidly as possible, providing the appropriate amount of information by the most appropriate means to achieve the required result. Above all, remember that engagement means a dialogue. To realize stakeholder value you must recognize their perceptions and understandings and be prepared to be flexible and reactive with your strategy as necessary.

Robbie MacDuff, Director of Public Affairs, Precise Public Affairs

Developing and maintaining effective and trusting relationships with clients is a key component of successful public affairs consultancy. Generally, clients do not expect their consultant to know as much or more about the issues they are seeking political communications support for, but it is crucial that the consultant quickly develops a detailed understanding of those issues so that he or she can speak authoritatively about them and understand the political and public policy initiatives that impact upon them. The consultant should always be proactive in communications with a client and in doing so be innovative in identifying ways to support the client's consultancy requirements. Being 'sparky' works well!

Malcolm George, Director of Marketing and Communications, EDS UK

Too many organizations seeking to influence the political process focus solely on the individual decision-maker relevant to their issue or case. Decisions are rarely made in a vacuum and decision-makers are often influenced by a wide range of stakeholders including civil servants, NGOs, industry bodies, trade unions etc. Organizations will almost always be better served by building a dialogue with, and gaining the support of, such stakeholders over a period of time, rather than focusing all their efforts on securing a one-off meeting with the ultimate decision-maker.

TRAMTIME

Working together on transport initiatives in Edinburgh, the challenge facing Weber Shandwick Scotland was how to make trams relevant to individuals to ensure that the legislation necessary to introduce trams back into Edinburgh would be passed successfully through the Scottish parliament. The tactic used to promote the positive benefits of trams to all groups was the theme of 'time' – saving time means greater productivity, easier accessibility and less time in traffic jams.

The implementation of the 'Time Machines' campaign was split into two parts and implemented in a carefully planned programme:

- 'It's tramtime' – an information campaign focusing on the benefits of trams, eg cleaner air quality versus pollution (eg one in four children in the Lothians is diagnosed as having asthma); faster journeys (eg being stuck in traffic costs businesses billions of lost revenue annually). The 'tramtime' campaign was rolled out two months before the consultation was due .to take place through mailings, media, advertising and online marketing. These were mailed to all audiences: the public, interest groups, stakeholders, political and media.

- 'It's talktime' – a public consultation process to obtain feedback and opinion on trams in general and specific route options.

Communications tactics were devised to most closely meet the needs of the target groups:

- Public – 125,000 'tramtime' leaflets were issued; 125,000 'talktime' consultation leaflets were produced; roadshow exhibitions were undertaken; public meetings conducted; a freephone number made available to call for information; a website with online response capability; and tactical advertising.
- Interest groups – received tailored e-mailing; presentations to key groups delivered; focus groups established to bring the experience and expectations of the interest groups to bear on the campaign.
- Political – presentations to cross-party groupings to explain the campaign; and e-briefings provided to parliamentarians.
- Business – received a 'tramtime' brochure; a business leader boardroom tour was rolled out; a 'tramtime' relationship manager acted as liaison officer with business; seminars held; an advisory panel established with business representatives; a dedicated website to link directly to company intranets; business champions helped to deliver the messages about the campaign to other businesses.
- Media – a media launch signalled the start of the campaign and ongoing media relations through broadcast, print and online were then conducted. In addition, an issues letter campaign was encouraged to ensure a continued media presence alongside endorsement articles.

In addition to this activity, a number of other actions were undertaken:

- Tactical advertising on the time theme 'it's tramtime'/'it's talktime' was used to promote key messages, meetings and exhibitions, website and freephone numbers.
- Freephone responses to queries and objections were dealt with daily.

- Community liaison groups were set up in key areas where the tram route was causing concern. Local resident representation met key team members to discuss issues and reach resolution. Amendments were made to the final routing as a result of these discussions.
- A 'traveltime' newsletter was produced at the end of the consultation.

The campaign and consultation were used to demonstrate that a credible scheme with public support had been established. The campaign could point to:

- 83.6 % of consultation responses showed support for trams;
- business leaders supported trams in media;
- heritage bodies were cautiously supportive – a major result in a heritage city;
- website hits averaged 46,000 per week (launch week 70,000);
- media tracking on positive/negative coverage (initially public weighted negative, then became supportive);
- each individual in Edinburgh had the opportunity to see or hear something about the consultation up to 14 times throughout the duration of the consultation (based on an Edinburgh population of 448,624 (Edinburgh Census 2001).

Edinburgh City Council passed the trams bills in December 2003 and they were introduced to parliament in January 2004.

This campaign clearly demonstrates the need to understand a campaign's various stakeholders and to deliver a strategy that recognizes their needs. It also shows that a consultation has to be real and recognize the needs of stakeholders if it is to be successful.

TATE – LAUNCH OF TATE MODERN

Tate Modern opened to the public on 12 May 2000. As well as being the first new national museum to open in London in a century, it is also the first national museum for modern art in London. The Tate communications team needed to ensure that the launch of the new Tate was covered sufficiently by both the national and international media to increase public awareness, understanding and appreciation of modern art. In order to reach this goal, it was necessary to make modern art more accessible.

There was also an international perspective as New York and Paris also have exemplary well-established modern art museums. Tate

Modern would be the first national modern art museum in London and, therefore, the international art world was watching Tate closely. The communications team had to certify that the opening of Tate Modern established the gallery firmly in the international art arena.

Unlike other major regeneration projects Tate wanted to make sure that the local residents and community groups were involved with and benefited from the new gallery. Only that way could they be seen as responsible and caring neighbours.

The campaign:

- secured the involvement of British artists;
- established why Tate is important and necessary;
- lobbied government to ensure Tate Modern entry was free;
- enlisted the support of high-profile endorsers and key members of the media.

In particular, a development officer worked closely with local residents and community groups, ensuring that they felt involved with and supported the project. Prior to the main press days, a private view of the museum for local residents and press was arranged.

The communications team recognized that to attract a wide audience to Tate Modern it was necessary to secure the support of television, the mid-market papers and crucially the tabloids, bearing in mind that the plans for the gallery were heavily criticized by the *Sun* when first launched in 1995. Actions included:

- Events such as the black cab drivers' preview to try to secure favourable coverage in the tabloids.
- The *Observer* did a special supplement to launch Tate Britain. *Vogue* magazine did a similar feature in May. *Time Out* filed a particular guide to the Bankside area and the *Sunday Times* Magazine covered all art lottery projects.
- Tate Modern secured a four-part documentary on Channel 4 on the architecture and building project as well as four art documentaries on BBC2. The opening by the Queen was covered live on BBC1. GMTV hosted their breakfast show from the Tate Modern.
- Working with PR agencies in France and New York, the Tate communications team was able to secure extensive international coverage and specialist art world press throughout the world.
- The creation of corporate identity and associated materials reflected 'brand values'.
- On the marketing side, six different adverts appeared across a range of media (including bus sides). A range of non-commercial

promotions were secured to support the marketing campaign, producing six million special coffee cups for Coffee Republic.

- The creative content of the campaign was enhanced by collaborations with British artists. A fanfare by Sir Harrison Birtwistle was commissioned for the Queen's formal opening of the museum. Tracy Emin produced a front cover for the *Observer's* British Art supplement and celebrities added glamour to the opening party. The opening show was broadcast live on the BBC.
- The Tate website was redesigned and upgraded prior to the opening.

The campaign's initial objectives were achieved and in some cases exceeded. The media campaign was successful in ensuring that the tabloids viewed the opening of Tate Modern favourably and coverage came from national and international outlets. Around 5.25 million people visited Tate Modern in its first year, a figure more than double that of their expectations. Over one million people came in the first six weeks.

The Tate Modern campaign shows how important it is to have a clear understanding of your audiences and also the need to work with a range of stakeholders.

Endnote

1. Manchester United TV (MUTV) is a subscription-only TV channel that broadcasts nothing but programmes about the football club.

6

Corporate social responsibility

Corporate social responsibility (CSR) is becoming an increasingly important part of the business and political lexicon but it remains unclear what it really means and how it impacts on an organization. CSR has grown rapidly, and relatively smoothly, over the last 20 years as increasing numbers of organizations – primarily businesses but also NGOs and charities – take up the banner of CSR in attempts to make their operations more ethical.

In relation to public affairs, getting your CSR right is very important as it will impact on your reputation. If others in your sector are moving forward with a CSR programme, then you also need to, otherwise you will be disadvantaged in political circles. If others are not, then this can present opportunities for you. Politicians, and the media, will reward those with good reputations and CSR programmes with a more favourable hearing or the possibility of being heard. In the event of a crisis a comprehensive CSR programme can also be used as a defence.

CSR can be used as proof of ethical behaviour and build goodwill amongst key stakeholders. For these reasons you need to understand CSR and how it has come about.

Beware of some confusion about terms in this area especially as some have started to use the term 'corporate responsibility' to try and move beyond a supposed perception that CSR only refers to the social elements of a company's behaviour and operations. As a relatively new part of the public affairs lexicon this confusion does not help matters and provides more ammunition for those who see CSR as just a 'flash in the pan', a fad whose time will pass quickly. The chapter discusses some of these opinions but it is clear from reading annual reports, hearing the speeches of leading chief executives and comments from respected business organizations, such as the Confederation of British Industry (CBI), that CSR is impacting on the behaviour of business and is being seen to make a positive contribution.

DEFINITIONS

The Department of Trade and Industry (DTI) sponsored Corporate Responsibility Group defined CSR as 'the management of an organization's total impact upon its immediate stakeholders and upon the society within which it operates. [...] it is about the integrity with which a company governs itself, fulfils its mission, lives by its values, engages with its stakeholders, measures its impacts and reports on its activities.'

Similarly, the British Standards Institute claims that CSR is 'a mechanism for organizations to voluntarily integrate social and environmental concerns into their organizations and their interaction with their stakeholders, which are over and above the organization's legal responsibilities.'

Martin Le Jeune prefers looking at corporate responsibility as an umbrella term 'for a positive relationship between an organization (usually a commercial body, but not necessarily so) and the societies/stakeholder communities in which it operates.'[1]

Looking more specifically at the corporate responsibility within companies, Patricia Peter of the Institute of Directors suggests that 'It's about having an effective board, a well-managed company and good risk and reputation management. Corporate responsibility and corporate governance are both elements of the board's overall role.'[2]

This last point is also instructive in demonstrating that CSR does not just include ethical behaviour externally but also internally – you have to ensure that governance structures are appropriate.[3]

Your range of stakeholders may be very large, as set out in the previous chapter, and could include:

- employees;
- suppliers;
- customers;

- shareholders;
- the community in which you operate.

From the perspective of public affairs, the government must also be included as one of those stakeholders. This will especially be the case for those organizations operating in highly regulated or very political fields.

MEASURING CSR

This is an area of much contention. There are a wide variety of ways in which CSR can be measured and ideas about what CSR should include. The United Nations Global Compact, International Labour Organizations (ILO), the OECD and many others' measures compete to show that theirs are the one true way of conducting CSR activity. This leads to confusion.

Many companies in the UK prefer to sign up to the Business in the Community (BiTC) system of benchmarking. BiTC provides a full checklist of areas that companies need to fulfil in order to be corporately socially responsible and then ranks the companies against each other.

Many companies issue CSR reports detailing their good work. Again, the form that these reports take varies enormously – from simple statements of intent through to full colour glossy brochures roughly approaching the size of *War and Peace*!

Much of this confusion has, in turn, led to a huge suspicion amongst the general public about CSR, its role and what it really means. In essence, the public does not believe that the companies do what they say they do and much CSR is deemed to be driven by the PR needs of the business. The media in turn are sceptical about CSR for CSR's sake.

At the heart of the debate is the need for real action. Organizations need to be able to show that all their talk of acting responsibly is backed up with real programmes and actions. Especially in the corporate sector any differences between the rhetoric and the reality will be ruthlessly exploited possibly by activist groups but also by competitors. This will, in turn, impact on your relations with stakeholders including the government.

Companies should choose CSR activity that relates to its core business and should not need to feel under pressure to adopt policies/actions irrelevant to what they do. In essence, they should adopt more of a 'menu' approach to measurement but ensure that everything they do is externally validated.

THE GROWTH OF CSR

The growth of CSR has several drivers including:

- The rise of activism – organizations introduced CSR programmes and reports in order to counter the damage inflicted on them – on reputations and, for some companies, sales – by attacks from activist groups who placed a spotlight on the behaviour of these firms.
- The rise of the 24-hour media – aided by the rise of the 24-hour news media, activists have been able to create an environment in which corporate wrongdoing has been given a high profile. Such stories make for compelling news but very often, good news CSR stories, of companies performing valuable roles in society, are not given such prominence as they do not make such exciting news.
- Societal change – it is now no longer appropriate for companies merely to make a profit, the way in which the profit is generated is under scrutiny as activists drill down into a business market behaviour, trade policies, employment relations, sourcing of raw materials, human rights, and for many, the most important, a company's environmental credentials. If a company was being exploitative in any of these areas then the activists would place pressure on them, through the media and other activities, making the issue public in order to force a change in behaviour.
- Changes in the corporate sector – companies have become increasingly dominant in people's lives. The rise of the brand and high-profile business leaders has meant that people are increasingly aware of the role of companies in society. This, combined with a decline in trust of politicians and a belief that modern governments lack power to make real changes, has meant that expectations of companies have altered. Add to this the rise of globalization and you see a much changed corporate sector over the past 30 years.

In many ways, the activists have the upper hand; they can attack companies and people believe their attacks. Companies can respond but people do not believe their responses. The dilemma for companies is that if they do not produce clear CSR statements then the activists will attack. However, if they do produce CSR reports then the activists can attack these also. A CSR report will benchmark a company's position so they must keep improving on this. If it does not then it is open to attack. If a company says that it behaves in a certain way then it must act in this way. If it does not, then it will be attacked. A further problem for companies is that very often they have tried to cover too much in their CSR activity reports – spreading themselves too thinly.

WHY CSR?

There are a wide range of reasons why CSR activity should be undertaken and there are now increasing numbers of studies that demonstrate the benefits that can be derived.[4]

- An Institute of Business Ethics report has suggested that companies with ethical commitments have 18 per cent higher profits on average than their competitors.[5]
- In a survey by CSR Europe and Euronext, 51 per cent of fund managers and 37 % of financial analysts said they would put a premium on socially responsible companies.[6]
- A Henley Centre report claimed that 60 per cent of institutional investors say that non-financial factors account for between 20 per cent and 50 per cent of their investment decisions.[7]
- According to a McKinsey Global Investor Opinion Survey investors claimed that they will pay premiums of between 12 per cent and 14 per cent in North America and Western Europe for companies with high corporate governance standards.[8]
- Research from the Chartered Institute of Personal Development (CIPD) and the Future Work Institute, 'Responsibility: driving innovation, inspiring employees', showed a clear connection between responsible business practice and a positive impact on the 'bottom-line' because it helps to attract, motivate and retain a talented and diverse work force. It also found that the employees believe that this type of workforce is more creative and innovative and this in turn enhances competitiveness and profitability.[9]
- Seventy per cent of chief executives globally agree that CSR is vital to profitability.[10]
- In Western Europe, 68 per cent of large companies report on what is being called the triple 'bottom-line' performance (economic, social and environmental factors) in addition to financial performance, compared with 41 per cent in the US.[11]
- According to BiTC, more than 70 per cent of business leaders believe that integrating responsible business practices makes companies more competitive and profitable.[12]

Reputation management is an increasingly important element of business activity. Many firms have established risk management committees. Barclays was one of the first companies to establish a 'brand and reputation' committee that puts reputation issues on a parallel with financial and operational risks. This is an explicit recognition that companies need to manage risks to their reputation more effectively. The UK mobile operator,

O_2, has assigned each of its board members with 'championing' an area thought to be a risk for the company.[13] A MORI survey among corporate communications directors of FTSE one hundred companies in October 2002 showed that 93 per cent believed that publishing non-financial information enhanced a company's reputation and made for better management decisions. A model based on the Fortune/Management Today's 'Most Admired' survey of 500 US and 250 UK companies showed a direct correlation between reputation and financial outcomes – share price and credit rating. It suggested that reputation, on average, accounted for 27 per cent of the FTSE 250 companies' market capitalization. According to a survey of US business leaders, financial analysts and journalists published in February 2004 a damaged reputation can take up to four years to be restored. According to a Harris survey of 800 CEOs in Europe and North America, three out of four international corporations have a corporate reputation measuring system in place, with the boards of 62 per cent of UK companies monitoring reputation.

It is becoming increasingly clear that organizations, especially companies, need to take CSR seriously. Yet this has to be balanced against reports that show that there is a clear scepticism regarding the way in which companies conduct their CSR activities:

- In a report by Tomorrow's Company, 'Redefining CSR', it is suggested that many companies see CSR as merely a box-ticking exercise driven by external pressures rather than by a genuine desire to conduct business in an ethical manner.[14]
- A survey of 56 leading lobby groups by Burson-Marsteller found that few believed CSR statements produced by companies.[15]
- Research published by the Salvation Army, (2003) *The responsibility gap – individualism, community and responsibility in Britain today*, demonstrated that 8 out of 10 Britons believed that companies should contribute to the society in which they operate but there was a serious concern about the emergence of a 'responsibility gap' that threatened the elderly, children, carers and other vulnerable people in society.[16]
- Christian Aid's report, (2004) *Behind the mask: the real face of corporate social responsibility*, suggested that businesses are using CSR as a front behind which they campaign against environmental and human rights regulations.[17]

Organizations are having to face up to these conflicting issues.

Companies are increasingly finding themselves liable to attack from activists. These attacks can take a wide variety of forms but the implications for companies are enormous. Activists are now increasingly looking not only to target the 'core' business, the aim of their attack, but also attack the network of financiers, insurers and suppliers on which the company relies. The focus of activists may not just be on the primary target but also secondary and even tertiary targets, and methods of campaigning, all with the same aim in mind. Many companies believe that they are immune from attacks from activist organizations. Whilst the most high-profile attacks are made on companies engaged in what may be deemed to be 'controversial' industries – animal testing, tobacco, extraction industries and so on – these are not the only companies that may be at risk.

Activist attacks, either directly or through the media, can impact on the 'victim's' public affairs programme. Government, politicians and regulators will not want to deal with an organization that is under attack, one that is seen to be behaving in an unethical manner.

Activist attacks can take many forms:

- Many activist groups and pressure groups will use existing political structures to try and exert pressure on government to take action against companies, eg by increasing regulatory or environmental sustainability requirements. Such lobbying is not just the preserve of corporations.
- Shareholder activism has placed pressure internally within a company as shareholders vote down motions at AGMs, and introduce their own, often controversial, motions. According to a survey by Watson Wyatt, one in two chairpersons of FTSE 350 companies said that shareholder activism had made them look again at their remuneration packages. The TUC launched a campaign at the start of 2003 to increase shareholder activism by pension funds and even the Association of British Insurers (ABI) believes that its members should play an active role on company resolutions.
- Many activist groups use legal recourse to attack companies. This is especially the case in the United States where there has been an even greater reliance on such 'class actions'. Greenpeace launched a High Court case against the loans made to British Energy and the High Court has permitted temporary exclusion orders to protect the UK branches of several Japanese companies that are customers of Huntingdon Life Sciences (HLS).
- The spread of electronic communications such as e-mail and the internet has meant that the power of activists is often in their homes. Companies can find their websites bombarded with e-mails, phones can be barraged with calls and networks of activists are becoming increasingly powerful as they communicate more easily, enabling quick and successful action often across countries and even continents.
- The use of people power through demonstrations and activities such as occupations often cause maximum disruption to companies. Such action is enhanced still further if the people do something shocking. A group of around 600 Nigerian mothers and grandmothers protested

against Chevron Texaco and forced them to promise jobs, electricity and other improvements to villages in their areas simply by threatening to take their clothes off.

- Many pressure groups are extremely adept at using press, marketing and advertisements, to increase the prominence of their cause and will often use these against companies. Viral marketing campaigns (those that propagate themselves normally through the web and by e-mail), International Buy Nothing Day, and the work by Ad Busters are all useful weapons for activity. Ad Busters produces provocative, clever and often humorous perversions of corporate ads to make their points.
- Increasingly companies have found that direct action has led to violent attacks. Activists understand their legal requirements and are often careful to work within, as well as outside, the law. Companies are looking to continue to exert pressure on government to tighten laws still further to protect their staff.

THE ROLE OF GOVERNMENT

Governments across the world have encouraged CSR activity. This can be understood as activists apply the pressure that government would sometimes like to put on companies but are otherwise concerned about frightening them away from investing in the country, and all the associated implications for jobs and regional policy that this would have. Activists can often say and do things that governments would shy away from and can apply pressure in areas such as workers' rights, environmental standards etc. As developments have progressed, governments are now faced with a situation where some serious decisions about the future have to be made in this area.

Until recently, governments have been unwilling to legislate in the area of CSR, preferring instead to let companies and other organizations feel their own way through. The debate has tended to centre around companies wanting to have a system that they can police themselves, and activists wanting more stringent requirements in place.

More recently, however, governments have been more willing to put formal systems in place. In the United Kingdom, the Department of Trade and Industry legislated on the introduction of Operating and Financial Reviews (OFRs) as part of the annual report of large companies. These would have contained information on a company's relationship with its stakeholders, its environmental and community impact, corporate governance (how companies are managed and controlled) and risk management. However, in December 2005 it was announced that

OFRs were to be scrapped. The move to include non-financial elements marked a significant change from traditional financial reporting. With the first OFR reports due to be published in 2006 the government move came as a surprise to many but was welcomed by a number of business groups.[18] Some companies already produce voluntary OFRs and the Accounting Standards Board in 2003 revised its 1993 statement describing it as 'a formulation and development of best practice, intended to have persuasive effect'. It is believed that with many companies already having spent a lot of time and money preparing their statutory OFRs, many will now produce them voluntarily. Add to this a 1999 amendment to the 1995 Pensions Act requiring trustees of pension funds to declare their positions on ethical, social and environmentally responsible investment in their statement of investment principles and the United Kingdom appears to be developing a fairly robust CSR setting. Whilst statutory OFRs have gone, companies still need to report on non-financial issues through Business Reviews, a requirement of the EU Accounts Modernization Directive, and the government remains committed to non-financial reporting: 'We believe that it is important for companies to report on non-financial issues relevant to the development and performance of the business, including, for example, environmental matters and human capital management.'[19]

It could be argued that the effort that has already gone into the establishment of OFRs has provided a benchmark by which to measure performance that companies will seek to exploit.

The London Stock Exchange Corporate Code now requires companies to include details of the systems they have in place to manage non-financial risk in annual reports. In South Africa, the Johannesburg Stock Exchange has incorporated the King Committee governance code that includes elements of corporate governance.

The European Union is taking CSR issues very seriously. Initially, the European Council meeting in Lisbon in March 2000 made a special appeal to companies' sense of social responsibility. Then in July 2001, the European Commission launched a Green Paper on CSR that was followed by public consultation. A follow-up communication, in July 2002, saw the establishment of the European Multi-Stakeholder Forum on CSR that brings together trade unions, employers' organizations, civil society organizations and business networks to discuss the way forward for CSR. The Forum is discussing the merits of voluntary and regulatory approaches to CSR. The Commission is also keen to explore, in more detail, the relationship between CSR and corporate governance. Whilst they are in essence different, in the broad public sense the behaviour of a firm both internally and externally can be viewed together. Five other European countries have already introduced mandatory reporting requirements – Denmark, the Netherlands, Norway, Sweden and France. These cover issues primarily related to environmental reporting but France has gone further in requiring environmental and social issues to be included in director's reports.

Following a spate of corporate scandals in the United States, the powerful Sarbanes–Oxley Act was put in place. This act was signed into law by President Bush on 30 July 2002. It is claimed by many commentators to be the most drastic change to federal securities laws since the 1930s. The act radically altered the regulation of corporate governance and reporting obligations. It also significantly tightened accountability standards for directors and officers, auditors, securities analysts and legal counsel. The act included:

- certification of financial reports by CEOs and CFOs;
- ban on personal loans to Executive Officers and Directors;
- additional disclosure;
- auditor independence;
- criminal and civil penalties for securities violations;
- significantly longer jail sentences and larger fines for corporate executives who knowingly and wilfully misstate financial statements.

An examination of parliamentary activity in the United Kingdom has also seen two high-profile attempts to introduce legislation, by Linda Perham MP (then Labour MP, Ilford North) and Andy King MP (then Labour MP, Rugby and Kenilworth). Perham and King also introduced motions into parliament to raise the profile of their calls to force companies to publish reports on the ecological and social impact of their businesses. Over 100 organizations, including charities, faith based groups and trade unions have come together to back these calls under the banner of CORE and have asked for laws to be introduced requiring companies to report on their social and environmental performance as well as creating a 'duty of care' for company directors similar to current health and safety requirements. CORE includes Amnesty International, Christian Aid, Friends of the Earth, the New Economics Foundation, Save the Children, Traidcraft and the Unity Trust Bank.

IMPACT OF CSR ON PUBLIC AFFAIRS

When considering your public affairs programme, CSR is becoming an increasingly important element. There are a number of reasons for this but they revolve primarily around the need to maintain a good reputation and trust among all your stakeholders.

Government and politicians will not want to deal with organizations who:

- do not treat their stakeholders well – especially their employees;
- do not follow the 'best practice' of their competitors or others in their sector – if others behave 'better' than you then your public affairs activity may suffer;
- have a poor standing in the community;
- suffer from criticisms from activist groups;
- suffer attacks from the media on a regular basis because of their behaviour.

It has to be remembered that political audiences and regulators rely on the media for much of their information about organizations and build their appreciation of organizations from similar sources as other citizens. These would include:

- the media;
- friends and family;
- other politicians/regulators;
- the views of the electorate/their constituency in the case of MPs;
- contact with the organization/details received from the organization;
- the behaviour of similar organizations, ie comparisons;
- activist organizations.

For those involved in public affairs the lesson is clear: get the communication with politicians right, ensure that it takes place early and build a profile with them. CSR can be a useful tool in the process of building a positive profile and also avoiding the creation of a negative profile.

This chapter is not primarily concerned with the development of a CSR programme but with its use in public affairs. As a general guide, however, there are a number of considerations for the development of a programme. It would be preferable that public affairs professionals are involved to help ensure that it helps to fulfil your needs, as well as others:

- Look at what the organization does well or badly – a starting point should be an assessment of current activity throughout the organization. Use the measures offered by reputable bodies to help you identify appropriate environmental, human rights and labour relations categories. This process may take place through a session involving all relevant people in your organization or by sending out a questionnaire for them to complete. For the CSR to really take root in your organization it requires senior level ownership, preferably at board level, but also needs to involve everyone at all levels of the organization.
- Identify stakeholders you need to talk to about your CSR activity – these can range from trade unions on the labour side, through to

representatives of the local community or suppliers. It has also to be considered that your stakeholders may not just be in one country.

- Once your stakeholders have been identified, a dialogue needs to be established with them. Ask them about their expectations, what they want to see the organization do, how it could improve, and share the results of your earlier work as an indication of the type of activity you see as necessary. Consider also employing outside auditors of this process as this will help to prove independence and, thereby, protect you from criticisms from activist groups.
- Communicate the results – once you have learnt about what you do, what you need to do and ensured that all stakeholders have played a role in this process then it is time to look to communicate this information. Options include:
  - reports – these need to vary depending on the stakeholding group with which you are engaging, ie avoid the *War and Peace* epics and keep the report down to a manageable length;
  - website – make documents available online and consider allowing online feedback to assist in the process going forward;
  - meetings – not everyone will want or be able to access documents electronically or have the time or inclination to read a report, so meetings in the community may be helpful;
  - other documents – do not confine your statements and commitments to just a CSR report, look to use other documents that your organization produces to reiterate the commitments;
  - a voluntary OFR – building on the work already put into writing them and the possibility that competitors may also publish them.
- Ongoing contact – use your CSR programme to work with all stakeholders on an ongoing basis. The process should not be a one-off event but should continue throughout the year.
- Evolve the programme – the programme should not remain static but should build year-on-year to be constantly improved and developed. If you rest on your laurels then your stakeholders will become disillusioned.

You can consider seeking media coverage of your CSR activity but it is generally the case that unless the programme is particularly innovative then you will not achieve coverage. It may be more useful to include reference to the programme alongside other coverage and other stories about the organization.

It should be remembered, however, that a good CSR programme is also about avoiding negative media coverage. If the media knows that you generally behave in an ethical manner then they are less likely to launch an attack. The same can also be said for activists. Do though remember that this is not a cast iron guarantee of being left alone!

The CSR programme can also be a defence if attacked. If, for instance, you are involved in an environmental incident, as part of dealing with the crisis you can also talk about the environmental work that you do and the protection activity in which you are engaged. This will help negate at least some of the attack. As described in Chapter 3, which looks at reputation and the media, preparation is essential when dealing with media, especially when looking towards potential crisis. CSR can play a key role in helping you get your positive messages right in advance of a crisis.

CSR can act as a very useful way to build relations with government and politicians or to help maintain existing relationships. In essence, they need to know about your CSR activity and especially any parts of it that are relevant to them. This is, of course, easier to convey to constituency MPs with regard to work in the local community, or to a sponsoring department that should take an interest in your industry in any case. Do not, however, be afraid to use CSR as a way to communicate with the wider political audience or others who may not have heard from you in the past. Your innovative CSR programme could act as an introduction to your organization and issues.

Look at your list of opinion formers, as discussed in Chapter 2 on lobbying, and aim to expand it, where possible. As well as the obvious politicians, consider contacting:

- business groups;
- local government;
- councillors;
- think tanks;
- charities;
- regulators;
- those involved in the development of CSR and who have a thought leadership role.

When putting together a briefing on your CSR programme for these audiences consider:

- what is new or innovative about your work;
- why they should be interested in your work;
- what lessons can be learnt;
- whether it can be applied to others in your sector as best practice;
- the nature of your programme;
- the steps taken to build it;
- the range of stakeholders engaged with;
- the future development of the programme.

When engaging in this form of contact you need to take feedback from your audience and, where possible, aim to incorporate their comments in your CSR programme. They too form a stakeholder group and their views should not be ignored. If you were to do so then you may find that these stakeholder groups become disillusioned and lose interest.

CONCLUSION

Organizations are having to take CSR seriously. There are a number of clear 'business' reasons to undertake it and the evidence is becoming clearer on this. Many, however, remain wary about CSR – they realize that it can be good for the business, its sales, employee morale and reputation but there is still confusion over the form of CSR and little clarity over what it really should entail.

Whilst CSR offers some very valuable public affairs opportunities, these are only obvious if the programme is devised with the right reasons at heart, not communications but ethics. You have to mean it and not just 'talk' it. A 'greenwash' will be hunted down by activists and the media and your reputation and political contacts will collapse.

A well-designed and well-implemented CSR programme that really relates to the activity of your organization will have the opposite effect. It will offer the opportunity to:

- build goodwill amongst stakeholders;
- enable the development of contacts, ie with government and politicians;
- offer protection from attack;
- enable positive messages to be developed in the event of a crisis;
- build and enhance reputations – for a business this can protect sales, share price, and profits.

Build a CSR programme you can be proud of and only then communicate it and use it in your public affairs.

Martin Le Jeune, Head of Public Affairs, BSkyB

Any company that embarks on a CSR programme hoping to boost positive coverage in the media is missing the point.

Not because gaining a positive reputation is in any sense antithetical to CSR – it can be a valuable and legitimate part of the business case.

But the secret of CSR communications success is to concentrate on your stakeholders and let the media tag along behind.

That approach obeys two of the oldest rules of communications in the book: third party endorsement is critical, and journalists are cynical. Better still, any decent programme should be tested in a frank dialogue with stakeholders. Then you have a strategy that is robust enough to sustain critical scrutiny and questioning by the media. It might not receive unalloyed praise, but it won't be rubbished through ignorance.

Adele Biss, Chairman, AS Biss

When it comes to shaping regulation or public policy it would be nice but unrealistic to think that the strength and legitimacy of a well-developed and well-presented case generally wins the day. But politicians have to balance many conflicting objectives so your arguments, supporting evidence and interests won't necessarily carry the same weight with them as do other pressures.

There is no force so hard to budge as a politician or official with a mindset. This is compounded if they do not make it clear to you that their position is, in effect, already taken. So timing is critical and the earlier you identify which way the policy wind is blowing the better. Always work hard on your case and communicating it well – that is critical. But as like as not you will need to exercise other levers too. Be sure that you know who to canvas for the most influential support – typically looking to the media, politicians, coalition partners, the law – and be skilled in the way you persuade them to pressurize effectively.

BT'S 'AM I LISTENING?' CAMPAIGN

MORI research revealed that BT's CSR reputation had plateaued. To improve its reputation, BT consulted with stakeholders and assessed the perceptions of its CSR activity. This resulted in BT focusing on young people as a key issue. Further research undertaken – 'Are Young People Being Heard?' – provided evidence of where communication gaps are greatest for young people. The key finding was that only 47 per cent of UK children and young people felt their voices were being listened to and acted upon.

BT's Social Responsibility Unit, together with Sinclair Mason PR & Corporate Culture launched BT's most ambitious social campaign in October 2002 with the first two years concentrating on helping ChildLine reach its goal of answering every call. BT's 'Am I Listening?'

campaign aimed to ensure that the voice of every young person in the UK is heard.

The overall objectives of the campaign were to:

- raise funds for ChildLine and provide operational support;
- help ChildLine move closer to its goal of answering every call;
- raise awareness of the need to listen to young people, and demonstrate the positive results when young people are heard.

There were several key business objectives:

- improve BT's CSR reputation;
- ensure at least 75 per cent of BT's 100,000 employees are aware of the campaign within two years;
- accrue tangible business benefits from the campaign.

The campaign established and supported fundraising platforms for ChildLine:

- BT Answer 1571 – BT Retail donated £1 for every person who signed up to their free answering service, 1571. This was delivered via an intense media relations programme and an internal communications plan.
- Customer survey – BT Retail sent surveys to each of its 19 million residential customers. For every survey returned, £1 was donated to ChildLine. Designed to take advantage of milestones and extend the news value of the initiative, the PR programme involved three phases: survey launch, £500,000 reached and £1million reached.
- Speaking Clock – As part of the BIG Listen week, BT ran a national competition with Newsround to find a young person's voice to be the Speaking Clock for one week.
- Seen & Heard – In partnership with the UK Youth Parliament, the campaign undertook a nationwide search for examples of young people who have succeeded in making their voices heard. Fifteen case studies were used in the 'Seen & Heard' report. These were presented to government, leading to a meeting with Margaret Hodge, MP for Children & Young People.
- BIG Listen – The BIG Listen week was the focal point of the campaign's calendar. The aim during the week was to raise funds and awareness of the need to listen to young people.

To date, the campaign has already raised over £2.9 million for ChildLine since April 2002 – the largest amount the company has ever raised for one charity and ChildLine is moving closer to its goal of answering every call. An additional 10,000 calls are now being answered each week.

The campaign has received over 1,600 items of coverage and 212,249,000 WOTS (weighted opportunities to see), representing the highest positive net effect of all BT related coverage across the company – 69 per cent of the total. Research shows 85 per cent of BT's 100,000 employees have unprompted awareness of the campaign, 83 per cent say that the activity has improved their perception of BT.

In addition, the business benefits are clear:

- BT Answer 1571 initiative: in one month take-up increased by 25 per cent.
- Customer survey: over 1.3 million customers responded, a higher response rate than would usually be expected and the findings allowed the company to target its marketing.
- Speaking Clock: there were over 2,000 entries and 4 million calls.

The campaign shows that CSR activity can help social as well as business benefits. Even a company as large as BT can galvanize support behind a single cause both internally and externally. The campaign stands out because it is truly holistic in nature: as well as communication/PR platforms, BT helps ChildLine with fundraising, research activity, volunteering, training, advising on use of communications technology and development of the charity's long-term strategy.

BREATHING LIFE

In April 2001, Centrica unveiled its 'Breathing Life' partnership with The Cystic Fibrosis Trust following a vote across its 30,000 employees. The partnership was formed 'to breathe life into the lives of those affected by cystic fibrosis and help raise awareness of this chronic condition.'

The aims for the 'Breathing Life' partnership were:

- to raise £150,000 for the Cystic Fibrosis Trust to enable the continuation of treatment for sufferers and to fund outgoing research for a cure;
- to create a better public understanding of Cystic Fibrosis and to promote the work being done by the Cystic Fibrosis Trust to eradicate it;
- to enhance the Centrica reputation and its brands as socially responsible and caring companies, whose management and staff fully support the work of the Cystic Fibrosis Trust;

- to improve employee satisfaction, motivation and pride and to give employees the opportunity and benefit from fundraising.

The partnership was designed to allow flexibility for fundraising activities across Centrica's individual brands while also providing an opportunity for coordinated activity across the total employee base. Employees were encouraged to come up with their own fundraising ideas as well as being offered the opportunity to take part in a comprehensive programme of fundraising events arranged by Centrica, in conjunction with The Cystic Fibrosis Trust. Scheduled fundraising events included the Scottish Gas Road Race, Lake District Challenge, Flora London Marathon, the World's Largest Bike Ride, New York Marathon and National Sausage Week.

The use of bubbles to signify the breathing life concept was an inexpensive and innovative way to raise awareness of cystic fibrosis as a respiratory illness. Its visual appeal secured coverage in *The Times*, the *Big Issue* and *Metro*, as well as many regional publications.

The simple visual idea was often utilized for regional fundraising stories, later followed by use of 'The Genie', a life-size depiction of the mascot for The Cystic Fibrosis Trust.

Local press showed great interest in the 'Breathing Life' partnership and extensively covered local employee fundraising initiatives, including activities as diverse as a mountain marathon, the world's biggest bike ride and National Sausage Week, the last of which was sponsored by British Gas. National Sausage Week was especially successful from a PR point of view as Cystic Fibrosis Trust secured celebrity chef Brian Turner to endorse the partnership and appear in the media photo call.

The positive coverage that the partnership achieved surpassed all expectations having generated:

- several hundred newspaper cuttings nationwide;
- radio interviews;
- extensive TV coverage.

A major aim during the (conception) formation of 'Breathing Life' was that this partnership would serve to raise awareness of cystic fibrosis as a disease and give the Trust a solid platform on which to continue their fundraising work and the search for a cure.

Thanks to the success of the partnership, the Trust had interest from future commercial sponsors, a testament to the enhanced standing that this ground-breaking partnership provided to a previously small, low-profile charity.

Equally, the partnership was very beneficial for Centrica – as the first integrated cross-Centrica charity initiative. It was a challenge to coordinate PR, both internally and externally, for 'Breathing Life', but it brought tangible results. Employees came together with a common goal and cemented working relationships across the group.

The total raised was over £300,000, double the goal figure of £150,000.

This programme clearly demonstrated how a CSR programme could deliver real benefits to a charity and also improve the reputation of the company involved. It has helped to enhance Centrica's community profile, raised awareness of the disease and promoted the work of the Cystic Fibrosis Trust.

Endnotes

1. Le Jeune, M (2004) Communicating corporate responsibility, in *Public Relations In Practice*, edited by A Gregory, IPR/Kogan Page, London
2. Maitland, A (2004) Good practice goes far beyond box ticking, *Financial Times*, 15 December
3. Maitland also goes on to describe how FTSE4Good, the ethical investment index, is looking at how governance issues fit with responsibility and how the role of boards can be altered to include these issues.
4. An excellent round-up of the financial benefits of CSR can be found in Lori Ioannou, Corporate America's social conscience, *Fortune*, www.fortune.com/fortune/services/sections/fortune/corp/2003_05cse.html
5. See www.ibe.org.uk
6. CSR Europe/Euronext (2003), Investing in responsible business: survey of European fund managers, financial analysts and investor relations officers, survey
7. See www.henleycentre.com
8. Global Investor Opinion Survey, www.mckinsey.com/clientservice/organizationleadership/service/corpgovernance/pdf/GlobalInvestorOpinionSurvey2002.pdf
9. See www.cipd.co.uk/subjects/corpstrtgy/corpsocres/responsibi.htm?IsSrchRes=1&cssversion=printable
10. Fifth Global CEO Survey, PricewaterhouseCoopers/World Economic Forum
11. PricewaterhouseCoopers/BSI Global Research Inc., 2002
12. see www.bitc.org.uk
13. Maitland, A (2004) Good practice goes far beyond box ticking, *Financial Times*, 15 December
14. See www.tomorrowscompany.com
15. See Denny, C (2003) Doubts over corporate consciences, The *Guardian*, 14 November
16. See www.salvationarmy.org.uk

17. www.christianaid.org.uk/indepth/0401csr/csr_behindthemask.pdf
18. OFRs were the subject of much lobbying from business organizations worried about the liabilities that they would bring. For instance, the Confederation of British Industry (CBI) were worried about the requirement that auditors would report on whether the OFR had been prepared by the directors 'after due and careful inquiry' – a high legal standard. This measure was subsequently dropped.
19. Rt Hon Alun Michael MP, 15 December 2005, House of Commons statement.

7

Conclusion

Public affairs is constantly growing and developing and, therefore, the skills required are likewise constantly growing and developing. As an example, the need to understand and work with the media has really come into its own over the past five years and so anyone involved in public affairs now needs this skills set. As CSR and stakeholder relations grow they become increasingly important skills and in years to come other 'topics' will come forward. Public affairs does not stand still and if those involved do then they will fail to meet expectations.

In an increasingly business-focused environment, those involved in public affairs have to be able to deliver a service that is in line with the needs of the organization. This has become apparent in two ways – the first is the demand to be able to measure success, and the second is the use of public affairs in a very obvious way to deliver improvements in an organization's 'bottom line'.

In terms of measurement, this has always been viewed as inherently difficult and simply not possible. To take this attitude is, however, to admit failure and if, especially, a consultant is to be successful, he or she needs to be flexible to the needs of companies and organizations and deliver ways of measurement. This measurement may take a number of forms:

- the number of opinion-former meetings secured;
- the number of meetings secured;

- the number of mentions in parliament or questions asked about the issue;
- coverage in the media;
- the measurement of reputation before and after the programme to see if there has been a demonstrable improvement because of the programme;
- the number of opportunities to input into policy identified;
- the number of inputs made into policy, ie number of consultation responses submitted;
- the number of secondary opportunities identified, ie opinion formers suggesting further contacts.

More difficult to measure is the impact on policy. Yet for some organizations the number of new business opportunities secured is a way in which public affairs can contribute to the 'bottom line'. This second way in which public affairs can deliver a service is particularly useful to those working with government on procurement issues. A good reputation and links with the relevant officials in a department places the organization in a better position to bid seriously for government contracts.

There is also a need for these organizations to maintain a good general reputation and also develop a serious and committed programme of corporate social responsibility.

ON A PERSONAL LEVEL

For those wanting to make a real impact in public affairs, apart from developing the appropriate skills required there are a number of other important tasks that await you!

- Make friends – be sure to maintain a good network of contacts and keep in touch with people. You never know when they may change jobs, may end up working alongside you or offer the prospect of work.
- Attend events – go to events that put you in contact with others.
- Join organizations – such as the Westminster Forum that offer the opportunity of hearing speakers and meeting like-minded public affairs practitioners.
- Professional bodies – ensure that you join a body such as the CIPR.

The overall aim is to network. There are a number of books dedicated to the art of networking but you must:

- always carry your business cards;
- be confident when you are introduced to new people and show an interest in them and their role, be sure to ask them questions;
- introduce yourself properly – first impressions count;
- when you are speaking to people give them your 100 per cent attention, do not look over their shoulders for someone more important to arrive;
- facilitate meetings and introduce people to one another;
- try to get a list of attendees before an event and identify those you most want to meet;
- remember everyone is in the same boat as you;
- try to remember the people you meet and their names if possible: you may want to write down names or add them to a contact list as soon as possible;
- do not drink too much – people will remember if you act foolishly in public!
- be prepared to follow up with those you meet, for instance offer to take them out for a coffee.

You can network at any event or gathering whether it is a breakfast seminar or a party conference.

Also on a personal level you should make an effort to try to set yourself and your organization away from the crowd. If you are able to offer something different, for instance in terms of expertise, or have a profile that others do not enjoy then this will help. Try to think about:

- building a personal specialization, ie in a policy area;
- building yourself a profile by speaking at events or writing books;
- using your networking skills to improve your contacts.

FUTURE TRENDS AND DEVELOPMENTS

As has been made clear throughout this book, it is important for those involved in public affairs to keep up with new trends and developments. Politics and communications do not stand still and, therefore, those involved in public affairs need to keep ahead of the game. By its very nature, some 'crystal ball gazing' is required when thinking about what may happen. However, some elements of the future of public affairs are already quite clear.

The internet and online communications

Whilst the use of the internet is now taken for granted, its uses in communications, for many, remain at having an online presence. This will come to be seen as insufficient, especially for political audiences. There is a great deal of work taking place, especially in the United States, on how online techniques can be used by voters to influence politicians; and yet most politicians have little idea about how to use online techniques, many MPs still do not even have an e-mail address that they use on a regular basis. The use of online communications techniques is largely led by activist groups who use them to 'attack' governments and corporations. They are more adept at knowing how and where to use new techniques of 'attack'.[1] There is much to be learnt from these activist groups and some corporations now work with some former 'attackers' to learn more about what motivates and drives them, as well as gaining an understanding of their methods of attack. 'Viral marketing' is a classic example of a form of communications that was developed by activists only now to be used by corporations in the pursuit of their aims. For those involved in public affairs, online communications need to be included as part of any strategy and the opportunities it delivers utilized to the benefit of the programme. As a simple example, an online petition can provide a clear demonstration of massive support for an issue but the step is to know how to utilize this support. Are there additional activities in which supporters can engage? Can you send automatic updates on numbers to those who you wish to engage with to show the continuing and growing support your issue has?

The 24-hour media

Even the media are not fully aware of all the impacts that this is having on the news agenda and even the careers of journalists. What is clear is that 24-hour agenda places additional burdens on journalists to create 'angles' and be able to help the story to grow and develop to keep ahead of their competitors. For those involved in public affairs, this means that knowing how the media fits within your campaign is increasing in importance as is the need to know to 'sell' your issue to the media in the first instance, help it to grow and develop and having the systems in place in case the story plays out in an unexpected way. Public affairs practitioners, therefore, need to know the media, in some ways as much as the journalists themselves do.

Devolution

There is an increasing emphasis on the empowerment of individual citizens and how to enable them to play an active role in the life of society. Some of this may be closely aligned with the development of online communications. There is also the possibility of new levels of government and of new bodies of representatives. These could take the form of regional government, new parish councils, or niche political parties that could exist only at a local/regional level and not impinge on the national scene. For those in public affairs, this means knowing politics at all levels and being aware and understanding what devolution really means for decision-making.

Global and international politics

Alongside devolution stands the possibility that as issues become increasingly global in nature, the obvious example being the environment, then much of the overarching policy will be set in global institutions. Implementation would then be assigned to each country. Placing such global bodies in charge of policy creates its own questions around levels of democracy and participation. For those involved in public affairs there will be a continued need to understand policymaking structures and where the pressure points in the system are.

Global clients

Globalization has brought with it the rise of companies that operate in an increasing number of countries. On the face of it this means that consultancies can have global clients of which they are but one part and for those 'in-house' they may need to turn themselves to issues in a number of different countries. For all those involved in public affairs it means being able, at all times, to be able to explain your own political system and what drives the strategy you are proposing. This is because your clients may have very little understanding about the politics and political environment in which you operate.

The rise of consultants

Since the 1980s there has been a rise in the use of consultants by companies. Public affairs is but one part of the consultancy landscape but its impact means several things for our industry:

- you have to be able to work alongside other consultants;
- you need to be able to able to work alongside existing 'in-house' teams, some of whom may resent your role;
- you must be able to demonstrate real benefit and make a contribution that the existing team could not.

OVERALL

Those involved in public affairs are continuously having to educate the market place about the benefits it can bring. In the UK especially, the industry is still relatively new and the discipline has still to make its way in to all organizations. This position will improve as public affairs professionals gradually take more senior positions and as they begin to take places on boards.

Public affairs is no longer the domain of several 'larger-than-life' figures but instead has become increasingly professionalized. How many companies would want to be associated with public affairs consultants who did not behave in a professional manner and were, therefore, in danger of inflicting damage on their reputation?

For those working in the industry, it is important that you adhere to a level of professionalism. If you work for a consultancy you should insist on regular training and be mentored properly. Also be aware that if you work for a progressive consultancy it may turn down clients that it does not feel comfortable representing and if it represents a company that you do not feel comfortable working for then you may be able to withdraw from the client team as long as you argue your position well and base it on fact rather than unsubstantiated rhetoric.

Several public affairs consultancies no longer exist. They have been taken over or have simply disappeared. Even the best ones can expect some flux in their position as the industry changes. Versatility in terms of the range of services offered is essential, along with the ability to move the agenda forward and offer clients something different. Every consultancy strives to offer this but not all succeed.

Delivery is all important. It is not simply the ability to discuss politics or communications but to supply a public affairs programme that delivers in line with requirements. Do not expect to be employed simply because of what you say you do.

Nowadays, the pressures on politicians have increased because the demands on government and the levels of scrutiny are so much higher. One way in which politicians can find out more about an issue, to inform policy and relive some of the pressure is through engagement with a number of organizations. Without public affairs, it would be more difficult for organizations to engage with a range of audiences, especially politicians. The public affairs industry plays a valuable role in the political process for a range of bodies.

> **Gill Morris, Managing Director, Connect Public Affairs**
>
> Why oh why do we have to go through it? It has to be both one of the worst and best experiences. Great when you win and lousy when you lose. We have all delivered the pitch performance of our lives, only to see the client of our dreams stay with the incumbent consultancy or worse. Relationship, research and rehearsal remain the keys to success in any pitch process. Being ahead of the game is the currency with which we trade. So make sure you know your stuff, make time to rehearse, generate confidence and show your winning streak.

PUBLIC AFFAIRS – A CHECKLIST

It is a somewhat difficult task to summarize a whole book in a series of points but if you were to remember only 10 things from this book then they should be:

1. Always be ready and be able to be to explain what public affairs is and how it can help.
2. Always grow and develop your skills.
3. Always act in a professional manner in line with codes of conduct.
4. Serve your client or internal audiences to the best of your abilities.
5. Make your arguments short and clearly understandable.
6. Ask yourself the questions that politicians or the media will ask...
7. and be able to answer them.
8. Provide solutions, not just problems.
9. Build and develop the reputation of your organization/client as a good reputation is beyond worth.
10. Never be afraid to air your ideas.

Endnote

1. See John, S and Thomson, S (eds) (2003) *New Activism and the Corporate Response*, Palgrave, London.

Appendix – codes of conduct

CIPR

Members of the Chartered Institute of Public Relations agree to:

i. Maintain the highest standards of professional endeavour, integrity, confidentiality, financial propriety and personal conduct.
ii. Deal honestly and fairly in business with employers, employees, clients, fellow professionals, other professions and the public.
iii. Respect the customs, practices and codes of clients, employers, colleagues, fellow professionals and other professions in all countries where they practise.
iv. Take all reasonable care to ensure employment best practice including giving no cause for complaint of unfair discrimination on any grounds.
v. Work within the legal and regulatory frameworks affecting the practice of public relations in all countries where they practise.
vi. Encourage professional training and development among members of the profession.

vii. Respect and abide by this Code and related Notes of Guidance issued by the Institute of Public Relations and encourage others to do the same (http://www.cipr.co.uk/Membership/ipr_codeofconduct.pdf).

APPC

Members of the APPC sign-up to the following code of conduct:

1. In pursuance of the principles in this Code, political consultants are required not to act or engage in any practice or conduct in any manner detrimental to the reputation of the Association or the profession of political consultancy in general.
2. Political consultants must act with honesty towards clients and the institutions of government.
3. Political consultants must use reasonable endeavours to satisfy themselves of the truth and accuracy of all statements made or information provided to clients or by or on behalf of clients to institutions of government.
4. In making representations to the institutions of government, political consultants must be open in disclosing the identity of their clients and must not misrepresent their interests.
5. Political consultants must advise clients where their lobbying activities may be illegal, unethical or contrary to professional practice, and to refuse to act for a client in pursuance of any such activity.
6. Political consultants must not make misleading, exaggerated or extravagant claims to clients about, or otherwise misrepresent, the nature or extent of their access to institutions of government or to political parties or to persons in those institutions.
7. Save for entertainment and token business mementoes, political consultants must not offer or give, or cause a client to offer or give, any financial or other incentive to any person in public life, whether elected, appointed or co-opted, that could be construed in any way as a bribe or solicitation of favour. Political consultants must not accept any financial or other incentive, from whatever source, that could be construed in any way as a bribe or solicitation of favour.
8. Political consultants must not:
   Employ any MP, MEP, sitting Peer or any member of the Scottish Parliament or the National Assembly of Wales or the Northern Ireland Assembly or the Greater London Assembly;
   Make any award or payment in money or in kind (including equity in a member firm) to any MP, MEP, sitting Peer or to any member of the

Scottish Parliament or the National Assembly of Wales or the Northern Ireland Assembly or the Greater London Assembly, or to connected persons or persons acting on their account directly or through third parties.

9. Political consultants must comply with any statute, Westminster or Scottish Parliament or National Assembly of Wales or Northern Ireland Assembly or Greater London Assembly resolution and with the adopted recommendation of the Committee on Standards in Public Life in relation to payments to a political party in any part of the United Kingdom.
10. Political consultants who are also local authority councillors are prohibited from working on a client assignment of which the objective is to influence a decision of the local authority on which they serve. This restriction also applies to political consultants who are members of Regional Assemblies, Regional Development Agencies or other public bodies.
11. Political consultants must keep strictly separate from their duties and activities as political consultants any personal activity or involvement on behalf of a political party.
12. Political consultants must abide by the rules and conventions for the obtaining, distribution and release of parliamentary and governmental documents.
13. Political consultants must not hold, or permit any staff member to hold, any pass conferring entitlement to access to the Palace of Westminster, to the premises of the Scottish Parliament or the National Assembly of Wales or the Northern Ireland Assembly or the Greater London Assembly or any department or agency of government. The one exception is where the relevant institution is a client of the political consultant and requires the political consultant to hold a pass to enter their premises.
14. Political consultants must conduct themselves in accordance with the rules of the Palace of Westminster, Scottish Parliament, National Assembly of Wales, Northern Ireland Assembly or Greater London Assembly or any department or agency of government while within their precincts, and with the rules and procedures of all institutions of government.
15. Political consultants must always abide by the internal rules on declaration and handling of interests laid down by any public body on which they serve.
16. Political consultants must not exploit public servants or abuse the facilities or institutions of central, regional or local government within the UK.

In all their activities and dealings, political consultants must be at all times aware of the importance of their observance of the principles and duties set out in this Code for the protection and maintenance of their own reputation, the good name and success of their company, and the standing of the profession as a whole (http://www.appc.org.uk/homepage.html).

PRCA

Members of the PRCA who come from the public affairs field have their own code of conduct:

1. In pursuance of the principles in this Code, political consultants are required not to act or engage in any practice or conduct in any manner detrimental to the reputation of the Association or the profession of political consultancy in general.
2. Political consultants must act with honesty towards clients and the institutions of government.
3. Political consultants must use reasonable endeavours to satisfy themselves of the truth and accuracy of all statements made or information provided to clients or by or on behalf of clients to institutions of government.
4. In making representations to the institutions of government, political consultants must be open in disclosing the identity of their clients and must not misrepresent their interests.
5. Political consultants must advise clients where their activities may be illegal, unethical or contrary to professional practice, and to refuse to act for a client in pursuance of any such activity.
6. Political consultants must not make misleading, exaggerated or extravagant claims to clients about, or otherwise misrepresent, the nature or extent of their access to institutions of government or to political parties or to persons in those institutions.
7. Save for entertainment and token business mementoes, political consultants must not offer or give, or cause a client to offer or give, any financial or other incentive to any person in public life, whether elected, appointed or co-opted, that could be construed in any way as a bribe or solicitation of favour.
8. Political consultants must not accept any financial or other incentive, from whatever source, that could be construed in any way as a bribe or solicitation of favour.
9. Political consultants must not:
   - Employ any MP, MEP, sitting Peer or any member of the Scottish Parliament or the National Assembly of Wales or the Northern Ireland Assembly or the Greater London Assembly;

- Make any award or payment in money or in kind (including equity in a member firm) to any MP, MEP, sitting Peer or to any member of the Scottish Parliament or the National Assembly of Wales or the Northern Ireland Assembly or the Greater London Assembly, or to connected persons or persons acting on their account directly or through third parties.

10. Political consultants must comply with any statute, Westminster or Scottish Parliament or National Assembly of Wales or Northern Ireland Assembly or Greater London Assembly resolution and with the adopted recommendation of the Committee on Standards in Public Life in relation to payments to a political party in any part of the United Kingdom.
11. Political consultants who are also local authority councillors are prohibited from working on a client assignment of which the objective is to influence a decision of the local authority on which they serve. This restriction also applies to political consultants who are members of Regional Assemblies, Regional Development Agencies or other public bodies.
12. Political consultants must keep strictly separate from their duties and activities as political consultants any personal activity or involvement on behalf of a political party.
13. Political consultants must abide by the rules and conventions for the obtaining, distribution and release of parliamentary and governmental documents set out by the institutions of government.
14. Political consultants must not hold, or permit any staff member to hold, any pass conferring entitlement to access to the Palace of Westminster, to the premises of the Scottish Parliament or the National Assembly of Wales or the Northern Ireland Assembly or the Greater London Assembly or any department or agency of government. The one exception is where the relevant institution is a client of the political consultant and requires the political consultant to hold a pass to enter their premises.
15. Political consultants must conduct themselves in accordance with the rules of the Palace of Westminster, Scottish Parliament, National Assembly of Wales, Northern Ireland Assembly or Greater London Assembly or any department or agency of government while within their precincts, and with the rules and procedures of all institutions of government.
16. Political consultants must always abide by internal rules on declaration and handling of interests laid down by any public body on which they serve.
17. Political consultants must not exploit public servants or abuse the facilities or institutions of central, regional or local government within the United Kingdom.

18. In all their activities and dealings, political consultants must be at all times aware of the importance of their observance of the principles and duties set out in this Code for the protection and maintenance of their own reputation, the good name and success of their company, and the standing of the profession as a whole.

(http://www.prca.org.uk/sites/prca.nsf/homepages/homepage)

EPACA

Members of the EPACA agree to the following:

This code of conduct applies to public affairs practitioners dealing with EU Institutions. As public affairs practitioners providing essential democratic representation to the EU Institutions, the signatories to this code (as annexed) are all committed to abide by it, acting in an honest, responsible and courteous manner at all times.

In their dealings with the EU institutions public affairs practitioners shall:

a. identify themselves by name and by company;
b. declare the interest represented;
c. neither intentionally misrepresent their status nor the nature of their inquiries to officials of the EU institutions nor create any false impression in relation thereto;
d. neither directly nor indirectly misrepresent links with EU institutions;
e. honour confidential information given to them;
f. not disseminate false or misleading information knowingly or recklessly and shall exercise proper care to avoid doing so inadvertently;
g. not sell for profit to third parties copies of documents obtained from EU institutions;
h. not obtain information from EU institutions by dishonest means;
i. avoid any professional conflicts of interest;
j. neither directly nor indirectly offer nor give any financial inducement to:
   - any EU official, nor
   - Member of the European Parliament, nor
   - their staff;
k. neither propose nor undertake any action which would constitute an improper influence on them;

l. only employ EU personnel subject to the rules and confidentiality requirements of the EU institutions.

Any signatory will voluntarily resign should they transgress the code. The signatories will meet annually to review this code.

EULOBBY.NET

Members of EULobby.net agree to the following code of ethics.

To help preserve and advance public trust and confidence in the EU institutions and the public policy advocacy process, professional lobbyists have a strong obligation to act always in the highest ethical and moral manner in their dealings with all parties.

The following 'Code of Lobbying Ethics' provides basic guidelines and standards for lobbyists' conduct.

This Code is intended to apply to independent lobbyists who are retained to represent third party clients' interests and to lobbyists employed on the staff of corporations, labour organizations, associations and other entities where their employer is in effect their 'client'.

Lobbyists are strongly urged to comply with this Code and to seek always to practise the highest ethical conduct in their lobbying endeavours.

Article I – honesty and integrity

A lobbyist should conduct lobbying activities with honesty and integrity.

1.1 A lobbyist should be truthful in communicating with Members of the European Parliament and with other interested persons and should seek to provide factually correct, current and accurate information.

1.2 If a lobbyist determines that the lobbyist has provided a Member of the European Parliament or other interested person with factually inaccurate information of a significant, relevant, and material nature, the lobbyist should promptly provide the factually accurate information to the interested person.

1.3 If a material change in factual information that the lobbyist provided previously to a Member of the European Parliament causes the information to become inaccurate and the lobbyist knows the Member of the European Parliament may still be relying upon the information, the lobbyist should provide accurate and updated information to the Member of the European Parliament.

Article II – compliance with applicable rules and regulations

A lobbyist should seek to comply fully with all European Parliament rules and regulations applicable to the lobbyist. In the context of their relations with the European Parliament, the persons whose names appear in the Register shall:

a. comply with all the European Parliament provisions governing lobbyists;
b. state the interest or interests they represent in contacts with Members of the European Parliament;
c. refrain from any action designed to obtain information dishonestly;
d. not claim any formal relationship with the European Parliament in any dealings with third parties;
e. not circulate for a profit to third parties copies of documents obtained from the European Parliament;
f. comply strictly with the European Parliament provisions regarding the Register;
g. satisfy themselves that any assistance provided is declared in the Register;
h. comply, when recruiting former officials of the institutions, with the provisions of the Staff Regulations;
i. observe any rules laid down by the European Parliament on the rights and responsibility of former Members;
j. in order to avoid possible conflicts of interest, obtain prior consent of the Member or Members concerned as regard any contractual relationship with or employment of a Member's assistant, and subsequently satisfy themselves that this is declared in the Register.
k. respect the European Parliament Code of Conduct.

2.1 A lobbyist should be familiar with the rules applicable to the lobbying profession and should not engage in any violation of such rules.
2.2 A lobbyist should not cause a Member of the European Parliament to violate any rule applicable to such Member of the European Parliament.

Article III – professionalism

A lobbyist should conduct lobbying activities in a fair and professional manner.

3.1 A lobbyist should have a basic understanding of the EU legislative and government process and such specialized knowledge as is necessary to represent clients or an employer in a competent, professional manner.
3.2 A lobbyist should maintain the lobbyist's understanding of EU governmental process and specialized knowledge through appropriate methods such as continuing study, seminars and similar sessions in order to represent clients or an employer in a competent, professional manner.

Article IV – conflicts of interest

A lobbyist should not continue or undertake representation that may create conflicts of interest without the informed consent of the client or potential client involved.

4.1 A lobbyist should avoid advocating a position on an issue if the lobbyist is also representing another client on the same issue with a conflicting position.
4.2 If a lobbyist's work for one client on an issue may have a significant adverse impact on another client's interest, the lobbyist should inform and obtain consent from the other client whose interest may be affected of this fact even if the lobbyist is not representing the other client on the same issue.
4.3 A lobbyist should disclose all potential conflicts to the client or prospective client and discuss and resolve the conflict issues promptly.
4.4 A lobbyist should inform the client if any other person is receiving a direct or indirect referral or consulting fee from the lobbyist due to or in connection with the client's work and the amount of such fee or payment.

Article V – due diligence and best efforts

A lobbyist should vigorously and diligently advance and advocate the client's or employer's interests.

5.1 A lobbyist should devote adequate time, attention, and resources to the client's or employer's interests.
5.2 A lobbyist should exercise loyalty to the client's or employer's interests.
5.3 A lobbyist should keep the client or employer informed regarding the work that the lobbyist is undertaking and, to the extent possible, should give the client the opportunity to choose between various options and strategies.

Article VI – compensation and engagement terms

An independent lobbyist who is retained by a client should have a written agreement with the client regarding the terms and conditions for the lobbyist's services, including the amount of and basis for compensation.

Article VII – confidentiality

A lobbyist should maintain appropriate confidentiality of client or employer information.

7.1 A lobbyist should not disclose confidential information without the client's or employer's informed consent.
7.2 A lobbyist should not use confidential information against the interests of a client or employer or for any purpose not contemplated by the engagement or terms of employment.

Article VIII – public education

A lobbyist should seek to ensure better public understanding and appreciation of the nature, legitimacy and necessity of lobbying in the EU democratic governmental process. This includes the right of any citizen of the Union and any natural or legal person residing or having their registered office in a Member State to petition the European Parliament.

Article IX – duty to EU institutions

In addition to fulfilling duties and responsibilities to the client or employer, a lobbyist should exhibit proper respect for the EU institutions before which the lobbyist represents and advocates clients' interests.

9.1 A lobbyist should not act in any manner that will undermine public confidence and trust in the EU democratic governmental process.
9.2 A lobbyist should not act in a manner that shows disrespect for the EU institutions.

SEAP

European affairs professionals are a vital part of the democratic process, acting as a link between the world of business and civil society and European policymakers. As such, these professionals must undertake to observe the highest of professional standards.

SEAP, the Society of European Affairs Professionals, aims to provide guidance thereon, by setting high standards. The SEAP code of conduct is the result of thorough discussions by SEAP members. It commits members to the rules laid down therein, sets standards and acts as a benchmark for all European affairs professionals and encourages third parties to respond to SEAP with their views on the code.

In their dealings with the EU institutions, European affairs professionals shall:

Article I – general principles

1. Act with honesty and integrity at all times, conducting their business in a fair and professional manner. They shall treat all others – including colleagues and competitors, as well as staff, officials or members of the EU institutions – with respect and civility at all times.
2. European affairs professionals shall not exert improper influence on staff, officials or members of the EU institutions.

Article 2 – transparency and openness

1. maintain the highest standards of professionalism in conducting their work with the EU institutions. When dealing with the EU institutions they shall be open and transparent in declaring their name, organization or company, and the interest they represent.
2. neither intentionally misrepresent their status nor the nature of their inquiries to the EU institutions nor create any false impression in relation thereto;
3. take all reasonable steps to ensure the truth and accuracy of all statements made or information provided by them to the EU institutions;
4. not disseminate false or misleading information either knowingly or recklessly, and exercise proper care to avoid doing so inadvertently. They shall not obtain any information from the EU institutions by illicit or dishonest means.

Article 3 – confidentiality

1. honour confidential information and embargoes and always abide by the rules and conventions for the obtaining, distribution and release of all EU documentation;
2. not sell for profit to third parties copies of documents obtained from the EU institutions.

Article 4 – conflicts of interest

1. avoid any professional conflicts of interest. Should a conflict of interest arise, the SEAP member must take swift action in order to resolve it.

Article 5 – employment of former EU personnel

1. when employing former staff, officials or members of the EU institutions, take all the necessary measures to comply with the rules and regulations laid down by the EU institutions in that respect, in particular with regard to confidentiality.

Article 6 – financial integrity

1. not offer to give, either directly or indirectly, any financial inducement to any official, member of staff or members of the EU institutions, except for normal business hospitality.

SEAP members shall uphold this code and all internal related procedures. In this respect, they shall co-operate fully with fellow members.

SEAP members agree not to engage in any practice or conduct that could be in any way detrimental to the reputation of SEAP or public affairs professionals in general.

Signatories accept that SEAP can apply a range of sanctions in case of non-compliance, ranging from a verbal warning to expulsion.

Index

NB: for endnotes *see* references/notes

Abramoff, J 8
ACAS 29
Accounting Standards Board 129
activists 124, 126–28
Acts of Parliament *see also* bill(s)
  Disability Discrimination 20
  Parliament (1949) 35
  Political Parties, Elections and Referendums, 2000 (PPERA) 32, 99
Adoption and Fostering, British Association for (BAAF) 60–61
Airbus UK 100
Al Fayed, M 6
America *see* United States of America (USA)
anti-fraud commissioner 16
APCO Europe 55

Barbour Griffith & Rogers 9
Barclays 125
Bell, Lord 44
benchmarking: BiTC system of 123
Bennett, K 100
Bill(s)
  Adoption and Children 60
  Communications 33
  Criminal Justice 58, 59
  Finance 38
  Financial Services and Markets 33
  government 33–34
  hybrid 34, 36
  private/private member's 34, 36
Biss, A 135
BiTC 125
Blair, T 26
Bland, M 81
BRAD 66
Brice, J 57
British Insurers, Association of (ABI) 127
British Standards Institute 122
Brussels 10, 11, 13, 16, 55

Budget, the 23, 38, 70
Business Ethics, Institute of 125
Business in the Community (BiTC) 123
business schools 91
Bush, President 8

Cabinet Office 16
Cartwright, R 112
case histories 58–61
  2001 census publicity campaign in Scotland 101
  British Association for Adoption and Fostering (BAAF) 60–61
  crisis management and child protection 76–79
  crisis management and domestic violence 79–81
  CSR: BT's 'Am I Listening?' campaign 135–37
  CSR: Centrica and Cystic Fibrosis Trust 137–39
  stakeholder relations: Tate – launch of Tate Modern 118–20
  stakeholder relations: Tramtime 116–18
  WWF and Traffic's Wildlife Trade Campaign 58–59
cash for questions scandal 5
Cass 91
Chancellor of the Exchequer 29
charities 8
Childline 135–37
Chime Communications plc 44
Christian Aid: 'Behind the Mask' 126
Citigate 6
civil service 28–29, 41
  and contact with lobbyists 16
Civil Service Yearbook 41
Clement-Jones, Lord xiii, 36
codes of conduct 15–16, 149–60
  APPC 15, 150–52
  CIPR 15, 149–50
  EPACA 154–55
  EULobby.net 155–58
  PRCA 15, 152–54
  SEAP 15–16, 158–60
Community Involvement, Statement of (SCI) 114
Competition Commission 28
Connect Public Affairs 147
Conservative Government 5–6
Conservative Party 61 *see also* websites
  Enterprise Forum 98
consultancy fee income 4–5
CORE 130
corporate governance 2, 129
corporate sector 8, 124
corporate social responsibility (CSR) 2, 46, 121–40, 141 *see also* case histories *and* definitions
  advice on 134–35
  and European Union 129–30
  growth of 124
  and impact on public affairs 130–34
  measuring 123
  media coverage of 132
  role of government in 128–30
  reasons for 125–28
  and stakeholders 130–32, 134
  studies on 125
council tax 47
Criddle, B 41, 45
crisis management 70–81 *see also* case histories *and* media, the
  advice on 79, 81
  and elected representatives 72–73
  holding statements 71–72
  and key groups 73
  and media training 74
  and monitoring events 72
  planning 76
  and stakeholders 72
  and the media 71–72, 73–76
Crown appointments 26
CSR Europe 125
Cubit Consulting 56

careers in public affairs 11–14
building skills and experience for 11
and CVs/application letters 12
early stages of 14–15
and phraseology 14–15
and sources of information 12–13
training courses in 12, 15
useful skills for 12

Daily Express 60–61
Daily Mirror 60
Davies, M xiii
definition(s) of
CSR 3, 122–23
lobbying 3–4
media 63–64
DEFRA 59
devolution, Scotland and Wales 6–7
difference, making a 7–8
Directors, Institute of 122
Dod's Parliamentary Companion 12, 41, 45
Duncan Smith, I 61

early day motion (EDM) 30, 37
economic consultancies 90–91
Centre for Economics and Business Research 90
Ernst and Young 90
KPMG 91
Economic Co-operation and Development, Organization for (OECD) 123
Economist, The 22
elected representatives 72–73
Electoral Commission 42
Ellwood, G 14
Euronext 125
European Affairs Professionals, Society of 15–16
European code 4
European Council 53–54
European Parliament 51–53
European Union (EU) 7, 10, 11, 51–55 *see also* European Parliament
Accounts Modernization Directive 129
Commission 13, 51–53
Constitution 53–54
and CSR 129
Council of Ministers 52
and Foreign Affairs Council 54
institutions of 51–52
lobbying in 51–55
Multi-Stakeholder Forum on CSR 129
and Permanent Representatives 52
Evening Standard 60, 61

Fair Trading, Office of 28
Financial Services Authority (FSA) 28
Financial Times 59
Fishburn Hedges 101
France and lobbying 10–11
FTSE 350 127
FTSE 250 companies 126
fundraising events/donations 31–32
future trends and developments 143–46
24-hour media 144
consultants 145–46
devolution 145
global clients 145
in global and international politics 145
internet and online communications 144
Future Work Institute 125

George, M 116
German public affairs market 10
GIW 6
global institutions 55–57
globalization and public affairs 8–11, 145
Government Affairs Group (GAG) Handbook 12

GPC 6
Green and White papers 33
Green Paper/papers 33, 85, 86
on CSR 129
Greenpeace 127
Greer, I 5
Guardian, The 13, 60

Hamilton, N 6
Hansard 14, 37, 42, 46
Hatcher, M 56–57
Heinz *et al* 5
Henley Centre 125
HM Customs and Revenue (HMCR) 38
HM Treasury 29, 33, 38
Home Office 59
House Magazine, The 13, 22
House of Commons 34, 36, 46
House of Lords 34, 35, 38, 46
Huntingdon Life Sciences (HLS) 127

Ian Greer Associates 5–6
Independent, The 59, 80
International Labour Organizations (ILO) 123
issues management 83–103 *see also* business schools; case histories; economic consultancies; polling organizations *and* think tanks
- advice on 100–01
- and building support 93–99 *see also* support *and* support-gathering strategies
- and clients' expectations 83–86
- and independent evidence 86–88
- practical steps for 99–101

jobs, placements and traineeships: sources and websites 13
Johannesburg Stock Exchange 129

Kallas, S 16

Labour Government 6–7, 20, 33
Labour Party 48 *see also* websites
- Industry Forum 98

Larkin, J 79
Le Jeune, M 122, 134–35, 139
Lewis, S 100
Liberal Democrat Business Forum 98–99 *see also* websites
Livingston Group, The 10
lobbying, courses and training in 3
lobbying 3–4, 8–9, 10–11, 19–62 *see also* case histories; definitions *and* lobbying contact programme
- advice on 24, 44, 55, 56–58
- domestic 56
- and European Union 51–55 *see also* European Union (EU)
- general rules for 57–58
- global institutions 55–57
- and local government 47–48
- meetings 45–46
  - and contact database 46
  - pre-briefs for 45
  - programme for 45–46
  - and searches 45
- and monitoring 21–24 *see also* monitoring
- objectives 24–25
- and policy 33–39 *see also* parliamentary process
- and policy-making in UK *see* policy-making in UK
- and public affairs 4–5
- reasons for 20–21
- in Scotland 48–50 *see also* Scotland
- strategy 39–40
- types of 21
- in Wales 50–51 *see also* Wales

lobbying contact programme 40–46
- briefing paper 40
- covering letter 42
- events 43–44
- meetings 42–46

principles for 44
Register of Members Interests 42
research 41
resources for 41–42
local government 11, 47–48
county councils 47
district, borough and city councils 47
levels of 47
parish and town councils 47
Local Government Commission 29
London Business School 91
London Tonight (ITV) 59
London Stock Exchange Corporate Code 129
Lord Chancellor's Department 59

MacDuff, R 116
McKinsey Global Investor Opinion Survey 125
McMillan, G 101
media, the 11, 22, 73–76, 124
24-hour 144
rules for dealing with 74–76
Media Directory (CIPR) 66
media relations 64–70
databases 41, 66
and letter writing 69
and press releases 68–69
and sell-in 66–67
media training 74
Mediadisk database 66
Milner 4
Mitchell, Senator G xiv
Moffett, T 10
monitoring (and) 21–24
audiences 21
government websites 22
media outlets 22
parliamentary matters 22–24
press releases 22–23
MORI survey 126
Morris, G 147
Munn, Meg (MP) 60

National Lottery Charities Board 80
networking 142–43
news stories 69–70
response to 69
types of 70
New Statesman 22
Nolan, Lord 16
Nolan rules 16
non-departmental public bodies 28
non-governmental organizations (NGOs) 8, 11
Number 10 59

Observer, The 60, 80
Ofcom 28
Ofgem 28

parliament 30–32 *see also* parliamentary process
all party groups 30–31
backbench committees/groups 31
constituency MPs 31–32
debates 37
Hansard 14, 23, 37, 42, 46
Lords Minutes 23
ministerial statements 36–37
Order Paper 23
PM's question time 31, 37
questions 37
select committees 30
specialist groups 31
weekly agendas 23
Parliamentary Commissioner for Standards, Office of the 16
Parliamentary Monitoring Services Ltd 24
Parliamentary Guide 42
parliamentary process 34–39
full legislative process 34–36
government bills 34, 36
paths of activity 36–37
parliamentary questions 30
people power 127–28

Personal Development, Chartered Institute of (CIPD) 125
Peter, P 122
Pinkham, D 9, 109
planning law 114
policy 33–39
  consultations 33–34
  and parliamentary process 34–39 *see also* parliamentary process
Policy Directorate 26–27
  advisers and appointments unit 26
  role of 26
policy-making in UK (by) 25–32
  10 Downing Street/prime minister 25–28 *see also* prime minister's office
  government departments 28–29
  parliament 30–32 *see also main entry*
  Policy Directorate 26–27
  sources/policy teams/think tanks 32 *see also* think tanks
Political Lobbying, Directory of 12
polling organizations 91–93
  Gallup 91
  MORI 92
  Opinion Leader Research 92–93
  YouGov 92
Private Eye 22
PR Week 12, 13, 15
press releases 22–23, 68–69, 74
pressure groups 128
prime minister's office 25–28
  and centralization of power 25
  Cabinet committees 27–28
  Communications and Strategy Unit 26
  Government Relations Secretariat 26
  key individuals in 27
  Policy Directorate 26–27
Professional Political Consultants, Association of (APPC) 12
public affairs in practice 2–3
Public Affairs News 13, 15
public relations 95
Public Relations, Chartered Institute of (CIPR) xiv, 4, 15, 79
Public Relations Consultants Association (PRCA) 4, 12, 15
public sector bodies 8

quasi-judicial bodies 29
Queen's Speech 23, 38, 70
Quinn Gillespie 9

references/notes 16–17, 61–62, 81, 120, 139–40
Refuge 79–81
Regester, M 79
reputation and the media *see* case histories; crisis management *and* media relations
reputation management 125–26
research studies/surveys 125–26
Richard and Judy Show 59
Riddick, G 5
Risk Issues and Crisis Management 79, 81
Roth, A 41, 45
Royal Assent 35

Salvation Army: 'The Responsibility Gap' 126
Schering 57
Scotland 48–50
  and considerations for lobbying 49–50
  and *Holyrood* 22
  and policymaking influences 48–49
  and Scottish Parliament 48–50
Scotland on Sunday 59
Shandwick 6
societal change 124
Spectator, The 22
stakeholder relations strategy 106–07, 141
stakeholder value 115

stakeholders 72, 105–20, 122–23 *see also* case histories
advice on 116
communicating/engaging with 111–12
and communications strategy 110
and CSR 130–32
effective 108
employees as crucial 109, 113
financial 107
geographical 108
identifying 107–09, 110, 115
key information on 110
media 108, 113–14
other types of 107, 113
planning communications 112–14
public 108
representative 108
understanding 109–11, 115
value of 106–07
Standards in Public Life, Committee on 16
Staples, B 55
statutory instruments (SIs) 35
student politics 11
Sun, The 59, 73, 80
support 93–99 *see also* support-gathering strategies
and potential allies 93–94
and profile building 94
and public relations 95
support-gathering strategies 94–99
membership of organizations 98
political parties and conferences 95–99
SWOT/risk analysis 25

think tanks 11, 88–90
Adam Smith Institute 88
Centre for Reform 88
Centre for European Reform 88
Demos 88, 90
Fabian Society 89
ippr 89
New Economics Foundation (NE) 89
Policy Exchange 89
Social Market Foundation 89
Today (BBC) 22
Trade and Industry, Department of (DTI) 122, 128–29
and Operating and Financial Reviews (OFRs) 128–29
training courses
Influencing Public Policy (CIPR) 15
Introduction to Public Affairs (CIPR) 15
Trayner, G 93
Treddinnick, D 5
Tribune 60

UK public affairs industry, changes in 5–7
United Nations (UN) 55
General Assembly 55
Global Compact 123
Treaty/Convention 55
United States of America (USA)
and Sarbanes–Oxley Act (2002) 130
lobbying in the 8–9
political action committees (PACs) 9
Public Affairs Council 9, 109

Vodafone Group 100

Wales 50–51
National Assembly 50–51
and policymaking 50–51
Waterstone's 80
Watson Wyatt 127
website checks 41
websites 22, 23, 95
Adam Smith Institute: www.adamsmith.org 88
APPC: www.appc.org.uk 12

Cass: www.cass-city.ac.uk 91
Centre for Economics and Business Research: www.cebr.com 90
Centre for European Reform: www.cer.org.uk 88
Centre for Reform: www.cfr.org.uk 88
CIPR: www.cipr.co.uk 12, 66
Conservative Party Enterprise Forum: www.enterprise-forum.co.uk 98
Demos: www.demos.co.uk 88
Ernst and Young: www.ey.com/global/content.nsf/International/Home 90
Fabian Society: www.fabian-society.org.uk/int.asp 89
Gallup: www.gallup.com 91
ippr: www.ippor.org.uk/home 89
KPMG: www.kpmg.com/index.asp 91
Labour Party Industry Forum: www.industry-forum.org/index.php 98
Liberal Democrat Business Forum: www.inbusiness.libdems.org.uk 98
London Business School: www.london.edu 91
MORI: www.mori.com 92
New Economics Foundation (NEF): www.neweconomics.org 89
Opinion Leader Research: www.opinionleader.co.uk 92
Policy Exchange: www.policyexchange.org.uk 89
Social Market Foundation: www.smf.co.uk 89
Society of EAP: www.seap.eu.org 16
www.cabinetoffice.gov.uk/propriety_and_ethics/civil_service/lobbyists.asp 16
www.parliament.uk/about_commons/pcfs.cfm 16
www.public-standards.gov.uk 16
YouGov: www.yougov.com 92
Welsh Assembly 50–51
Westminster and Whitehall 5, 11
When It Hits The Fan 81
White Papers 85, 86
Who's Who in Public Affairs 12
wildlife and Metropolitan Police Wildlife Crime Unit 59
Wildlife Trade Campaign 58–59
Wilson, H 19, 25
working for an MP 11
World Bank 55, 56
World Trade Organization (WTO) 55, 56
World Wildlife Fund (WWF) 58–59
and TRAFFIC 58–59
Control of Trade in Endangered Species (COTES) 58

Zetter, L 24

The *PR in Practice* series

Published in association with 

ISBN 10: 0 7494 4823 7
ISBN 13: 978 0 7494 4823 3
Paperback 2007

ISBN 10: 0 7494 3948 3
ISBN 13: 978 0 7494 3948 4
Paperback 2005

ISBN 10: 0 7494 4380 4
ISBN 13: 978 0 7494 4380 1
Paperback 2005

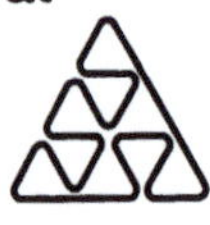

The *PR in Practice* series

Published in association with 

ISBN 10: 0 7494 2991 7
ISBN 13: 978 0 7494 2991 1
Paperback 2000

ISBN 10: 0 7494 4072 4
ISBN 13: 978 0 7494 4072 5
Paperback 2003

ISBN 10: 0 7494 3381 7
ISBN 13: 978 0 7494 3381 9
Paperback 2003

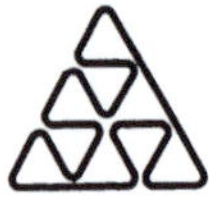

Printed in Great Britain
by Amazon.co.uk, Ltd.,
Marston Gate.